POCKET BIBLE

POCKET
BIBLE
Collection

Scriptures to Renew Your Mind
And Change Your Life

Harrison House
Tulsa, Oklahoma

15 14 13 12   5 4 3 2 1

The Pocket Bible Collection
ISBN: 978-1-60683-683-5

Copyright © 1995, 2003, 2012 by Harrison House, LLC.
Tulsa, OK 74145

TABLE OF CONTENTS

INTRODUCTION

Paul describes the spirit of faith in 2 Corinthians 4:13 as believing and speaking God's Word: It is written: 'I believed; and therefore I have spoken.' With that same spirit of faith we also believe and therefore speak" (NIV).

Faith is believing and speaking what God says in the face of natural circumstances, reports, or diagnoses. Faith is putting agreement with the higher report of God's Word. God will not change His mind about the promises of His Word. They will become a reality in the life of the person who is willing to believe and speak His Word as the highest standard of truth.

To put agreement with God's Word in the face of sickness or disease, faith believes and speaks, "By Jesus' stripes I am healed." (Isaiah 53:5; I Peter 2:24.) In the face of mental torment, faith believes and speaks, "I have perfect peace because my mind is focused on the Lord." (Isaiah 26:3.) "I am far from oppression, and fear and terror will not come near me." (Isaiah 54:14.) In the face of lack, faith believes and speaks, "God supplies my every need according to His riches in glory by Christ

Jesus." (Philippians 4:19.) "God's blessings make me rich, and He adds no sorrow

with it." (Proverbs 10:22.) In the face of anxiety, faith believes and speaks, "I cast every care, worry, and anxiety upon the Lord." (I Peter 5:7.)

The Pocket Bible Collection contains examples which you can follow of faith in action from biblical accounts in both the Old and New Testaments. You will rise to a new level as you meditate upon the principles of faith presented in the Scriptures contained in this Pocket Bible Collection. As a result, you will be better equipped to whip every challenge and overcome every hurdle, regardless of its complexity.

Because of the input of these power-packed, resurrection words, life will flow from your heart out through your lips. New heights and new victories—both spiritually and naturally—will be yours!

Prayer

Father, thank You for Your Word which is infused with the resurrection life of Your Son, Jesus.

As I take daily doses of the spiritual food contained in this Pocket Bible Collection, help me to rise to a new level of victory, triumph, abundant joy, and prosperity of spirit, soul, and body.

Thank You, Holy Spirit, for quickening my eyes to see as Jesus sees; to hear as Jesus hears; to discern as He discerns; to speak as He speaks; to love as He loves; to be immovable in the face of any challenge, fully confident that God's Word will prevail.

Help me to imitate You accurately, Lord Jesus, in my every thought, word, and action, in Your name I pray. Amen.

Faith Scriptures
Old Testament

And Abram believed the Lord, and the Lord counted him as righteous because of his faith.

Genesis 15:6 NLT

When Abram was ninety-nine years old, the Lord appeared to him and said, "I am God Almighty; walk before me faithfully and be blameless. Then I will make my covenant between me and you and will greatly increase your numbers."

Abram fell facedown and God said to him, "As for me, this is my covenant with you: You will be the father of many nations. No longer will you be called Abram; your name will be Abraham, for I have made you a father of many nations. I will make you very fruitful; I will make nations of you, and kings will come from you. I will establish my covenant as an everlasting covenant between me and you and your descendants after you for the generations to come, to be your God and the

God of your descendants after you. The whole land of Canaan, where you now reside as a foreigner, I will give as an everlasting possession to you and your descendants after you; and I will be their God."

Then God said to Abraham, "As for you, you must keep my covenant, you and your descendants after you for the generations to come."

Genesis 17:1-9 NIV

Know, recognize, and understand therefore that the Lord your God, He is God, the faithful God, Who keeps covenant and steadfast love and mercy with those who love Him and keep His commandments, to a thousand generations.

Deuteronomy 7:9 AMP

Now Jericho was securely shut up because of the children of Israel; none went out, and none came in. And the LORD said to Joshua: "See! I have given Jericho into your hand, its king, and the mighty men of valor. You shall march around the city, all you men of war; you shall go all around the city once. This you shall do six days. And seven priests shall bear seven trumpets of rams' horns before the ark. But the seventh day you shall march around the city seven times, and the priests shall blow the trumpets. It shall come to pass, when they make a long blast with the ram's horn, and when you hear the sound of the trumpet, that all the people shall shout with a great shout; then the wall of the city will fall down flat. And the people shall go up every man straight before him."

Then Joshua the son of Nun called the priests and said to them, "Take up the ark of the covenant, and let seven priests bear seven trumpets of rams' horns before the ark of the LORD." And he said to the people, "Proceed, and march around the city, and let him who is armed advance before the ark of the LORD."

So it was, when Joshua had spoken to the people, that the seven priests bearing the seven trumpets of rams' horns before the LORD advanced and blew the trumpets, and the ark of the covenant of the LORD followed them. The armed men went before the priests who blew the trumpets, and the rear guard came after the ark, while the priests continued blowing the trumpets. Now Joshua had commanded the people, saying, "You shall not shout or make any noise with your voice, nor shall a word proceed out of your mouth, until the day I say to you, 'Shout!' Then you shall shout." So he had the ark of the LORD circle the city, going around it once. Then they came into the camp and lodged in the camp.

And Joshua rose early in the morning, and the priests took up the ark of the LORD. Then seven priests bearing seven trumpets of rams' horns before the ark of the LORD went on continually and blew with the trumpets. And the armed men went before them. But the rear guard came after the ark of the LORD, while

the priests continued blowing the trumpets. And the second day they marched around the city once and returned to the camp. So they did six days.

But it came to pass on the seventh day that they rose early, about the dawning of the day, and marched around the city seven times in the same manner. On that day only they marched around the city seven times. And the seventh time it happened, when the priests blew the trumpets, that Joshua said to the people: "Shout, for the LORD has given you the city! Now the city shall be doomed by the LORD to destruction, it and all who are in it. Only Rahab the harlot shall live, she and all who are with her in the house, because she hid the messengers that we sent. And you, by all means abstain from the accursed things, lest you become accursed when you take of the accursed things, and make the camp of Israel a curse, and trouble it. But all the silver and gold, and vessels of bronze and iron, are consecrated to the LORD; they shall come into the treasury of the LORD."

So the people shouted when the priests blew the trumpets. And it happened when the people heard the sound of the trumpet, and the people shouted with a great shout, that the wall fell down flat. Then the people went up into the city, every man straight before him, and they took the city.

Joshua 6:1-20 NKJV

If you decide that it's a bad thing to worship God, then choose a god you'd rather serve – and do it today. Choose one of the gods your ancestors worshiped from the country beyond The River, or one of the gods of the Amorites, on whose land you're now living. As for me and my family, we'll worship God."

Joshua 24:15 MSG

David said to the Philistine, "You come against me with sword and spear and javelin, but I come against you in the name of the LORD Almighty, the God of the armies of Israel, whom you have defied. This day the LORD will deliver you into my hands, and I'll strike you down and cut off your head. This very day I will give the carcasses of the Philistine army to the birds and the wild animals, and the whole world will know that there is a God in Israel. All those gathered here will know that it is not by sword or spear that the LORD saves; for the battle is the LORD's, and he will give all of you into our hands."

As the Philistine moved closer to attack him, David ran quickly toward the battle line to meet him. Reaching into his bag and taking out a stone, he slung it and struck the Philistine on the forehead. The stone sank into his forehead, and he fell face down on the ground.

So David triumphed over the Philistine with a sling and a stone; without a sword in his hand he struck down the Philistine and killed him.

David ran and stood over him. He took hold of the Philistine's sword and drew it from the sheath. After he killed him, he cut off his head with the sword.

When the Philistines saw that their hero was dead, they turned and ran.

I Samuel 17:45-51 NIV

One day Elisha went to Shunem. And a well-to-do woman was there, who urged him to stay for a meal. So whenever he came by, he stopped there to eat. She said to her husband, "I know that this man who often comes our way is a holy man of God. Let's make a small room on the roof and put in it a bed and a table, a chair and a lamp for him. Then he can stay there whenever he comes to us."

One day when Elisha came, he went up to his room and lay down there. He said to his servant Gehazi, "Call the Shunammite." So he called her, and she stood before him. Elisha said to him, "Tell her, 'You have gone to all this trouble for us. Now what can be done for you? Can we speak on your behalf to the king or the commander of the army?'"

She replied, "I have a home among my own people."

"What can be done for her?" Elisha asked.

Gehazi said, "She has no son, and her husband is old."

Then Elisha said, "Call her." So he called her, and she stood in the doorway. "About this time next year," Elisha said, "you will hold a son in your arms."

"No, my lord!" she objected. "Please, man of God, don't mislead your servant!"

But the woman became pregnant, and the next year about that same time she gave birth to a son, just as Elisha had told her.

The child grew, and one day he went out to his father, who was with the reapers. He said to his father, "My head! My head!".

His father told a servant, "Carry him to his mother." After the servant had lifted him up and carried him to his mother, the boy sat on her lap until noon, and then he died. She went up and laid him on the bed of the man of God, then shut the door and went out.

She called her husband and said, "Please send me one of the servants and a donkey so I can go to the man of God quickly and return."

"Why go to him today?" he asked. "It's not the New Moon or the Sabbath."

"That's all right," she said.

She saddled the donkey and said to her servant, "Lead on; don't slow down for me unless I tell you." So she set out and came to the man of God at Mount Carmel.

When he saw her in the distance, the man of God said to his servant Gehazi, "Look! There's the Shunammite! Run to meet her and ask her, 'Are you all right? Is your husband all right? Is your child all right?'"

"Everything is all right," she said.

When she reached the man of God at the mountain, she took hold of his feet. Gehazi came over to push her away, but the man of God said, "Leave her alone! She is in bitter distress, but the LORD has hidden it from me and has not told me why."

"Did I ask you for a son, my lord?" she said. "Didn't I tell you, 'Don't raise my hopes'?"

Elisha said to Gehazi, "Tuck your cloak into your belt, take my staff in your hand and run. Don't greet anyone you meet, and if anyone greets you, do not answer. Lay my staff on the boy's face."

But the child's mother said, "As surely as the LORD lives and as you live, I will not leave you." So he got up and followed her.

Gehazi went on ahead and laid the staff on the boy's face, but there was no sound or response. So Gehazi went back to meet Elisha and told him, "The boy has not awakened."

When Elisha reached the house, there was the boy lying dead on his couch. He went in, shut the door on the two of them and prayed to the LORD. Then he got on the bed and lay on the boy, mouth to mouth, eyes to eyes, hands to hands. As he stretched himself out on him, the boy's body grew warm. Elisha turned away and walked back and forth in the room and then got on the bed and stretched out on him once more. The boy sneezed seven times and opened his eyes.

Elisha summoned Gehazi and said, "Call the Shunammite." And he did. When she came, he said, "Take your son." She came in, fell at his feet and bowed to the ground. Then she took her son and went out.

2 Kings 4:8-37 NIV

I know the Lord is always with me. I will not be shaken, for he is right beside me.

Psalm 16:8 NLT

For by You I can run through a troop, and by my God I can leap over a wall.

Psalm 18:29 AMP

Oh, love the Lord, all you His saints! For the Lord preserves the faithful, and fully repays the proud person.

Psalm 31:23 NKJV

Commit everything you do to the Lord. Trust him, and he will help you.

Psalm 37:5 NLT

I waited patiently for the Lord; he turned to me and heard my cry.

Psalm 40:1 NIV

Nevertheless, My loving-kindness will I not break off from

him, nor allow My faithfulness to fail (to lie and be false to him).

My covenant will I not break or profane, nor alter the thing that is gone out of My lips.

Psalm 89:33-34 AMP

This I declare about the Lord: He alone is my refuge, my place of safety; he is my God, and I trust him.

Psalm 91:2 NLT

Forever, O Lord, thy word is settled in heaven.

Thy faithfulness is unto all generations.

Psalm 119:89,90 KJV

I wait for the Lord, my whole being waits, and in his word I put my hope.

Psalm 130:5 NIV

Lean on, trust in, and be confident in the Lord with all your heart and mind and do not rely on your insight or understanding.

In all your ways know, recognize, and acknowledge Him, and He will direct and make straight and plain your paths.

Proverbs 3:5-6 AMP

When you lie down, you won't be afraid; when you lie down, you will sleep in peace. You won't be afraid of sudden trouble; you won't fear the ruin that comes to the wicked, because the Lord will keep you safe. He will keep you from being trapped.

Proverbs 3:24-26 NCV

A faithful person will be richly blessed.

Proverbs 28:20 NIV

If you do not stand firm in your faith, you will not stand at all.

Isaiah 7:9 NIV

You, Lord, give true peace to those who depend on you, because they trust you.

So, trust the Lord always, because he is our Rock forever.

Isaiah 26:3-4 NCV

The grass withers, the flower fades, but the word of our God stands forever.

Isaiah 40:8 NIV

But he was wounded for the wrong we did; he was crushed for the evil we did. The punishment, which made us well, was given to him, and we are healed because of his wounds.

Isaiah 53:5 NCV

The same thing is true of the words I speak. They will not return to me empty. They make the things happen hat I want to happen, and they succeed in doing what I send them to do.

So you will go out with joy and be led out in peace. The mountains and hills will burst into song before you, and all the trees in the fields will clap their hands.

Isaiah 55:11-12 NCV

Then the Lord said to me, "You have seen well, for I am ready to perform My word."

Jeremiah 1:12 NKVJ

I am alert and active, watching over My word to perform it.

Jeremiah 1:12 AMP

God's loyal love couldn't have run out, his merciful love

couldn't have dried up.

They're created new every morning. How great your faithfulness!

Lamentations 3:22-23 MSG

For I am the Lord; I will speak, and the word that I shall speak shall come to pass;

Ezekiel 12:25

Shadrach, Meshach, and Abednego replied, "O Nebuchadnezzar, we do not need to defend ourselves before you. If we are thrown into the blazing furnace, the God whom we serve is able to save us. He will rescue us from your power, Your Majesty. But

even if he doesn't, we want to make it clear to you, Your Majesty, that we will never serve your gods or worship the gold statue you have set up."

Daniel 3:16-18 NLT

But the just shall live by his faith.

Habakkuk 2:4

The righteous man trusts in me, and lives!

Habakkuk 2:4b TLB

New Testament

And when you pray, do not keep on babbling like pagans, for they think they will be heard because of their many words. Do not be like them, for your Father knows what you need before you ask him.

Matthew 6:7-8 NIV

"Therefore I tell you, do not worry about your life, what you will eat or drink; or about your body, what you will wear. Is not life more than food, and the body more than clothes? Look at the birds of the air; they do not sow or reap or store away in barns, and yet your heavenly Father feeds them. Are you not much more valuable than they? Can any one of you by worrying add a single hour to your life?

"And why do you worry about clothes? See how the flowers of the field grow. They do not labor or spin. Yet I tell you that not even Solomon in all his splendor was dressed like one of these. If that is how God clothes the grass of the field, which is here today and tomorrow is thrown into the fire, will he not much more clothe you—you of little faith? So do not worry, saying, 'What shall we eat?' or 'What shall we drink?' or 'What shall we wear?' For the pagans run after all these things, and your heavenly Father knows that you need them. But seek first his kingdom and his righteousness, and all these things will be given to you as well. Therefore do not worry about tomorrow, for tomorrow will worry about itself. Each day has enough trouble of its own.

Matthew 6:25-34 NIV

Keep on asking and it will be given you; keep on seeking and you will find; keep on knocking (reverently) and (the door) will be opened to you.

For everyone who keeps on asking receives; and he who keeps on seeking finds; and to him who keeps on knowing, (the door) will be opened.

Matthew 7:7-8 AMP

"Everyone then who hears these words of mine and puts them into practice is like a sensible man who builds his house on the rock. Down came the rain and up came the floods, while the winds blew and roared upon that house—and it did not fall because its foundations were on the rock.

"And everyone who hears these words of mine and does not follow them can be compared with a foolish man who built his house on sand. Down came the rain and up came the floods, while the winds blew and battered that house till it collapsed, and fell with a great crash."

Matthew 7:24-27 Phillips

Now when Jesus had entered Capernaum, a centurion came to Him, pleading with Him, saying, "Lord, my servant is lying at home paralyzed, dreadfully tormented."

And Jesus said to him, "I will come and heal him."

The centurion answered and said, "Lord, I am not worthy that You should come under my roof. But only speak a word, and my servant will be healed. For I also am a man under authority, having soldiers under me. And I say to this one, 'Go,' and he goes; and to another, 'Come,' and he comes; and to my servant, 'Do this,' and he does it."

When Jesus heard it, He marveled, and said to those who followed, "Assuredly, I say to you, I have not found such great faith, not even in Israel! And I say to you that many will come from east and west, and sit down with Abraham, Isaac, and Jacob in the kingdom of heaven. But the sons of the kingdom will be cast out into outer darkness. There will be weeping and

gnashing of teeth." Then Jesus said to the centurion, "Go your

way; and as you have believed, so let it be done for you."
And his servant was healed that same hour.

Matthew 8:5-13 NKJV

And when he was entered into a ship, his disciples followed
him. And, behold, there arose a great tempest in the sea, insomuch that the ship was covered with the waves: but he was
asleep.

And his disciples came to him, and awoke him, saying, Lord,
save us: we perish.

And he saith unto them, Why are ye fearful, O ye of little
faith? Then he arose, and rebuked the winds and the sea; and
there was a great calm.

But the men marveled, saying, "What manner of man is this,
that even the winds and the sea obey him!

Matthew 8:23-27

Then behold, they brought to Him a paralytic lying on a bed.
When Jesus saw their faith, He said to the paralytic, "Son, be of
good cheer; your sins are forgiven you."

And at once some of the scribes said within themselves, "This Man blasphemes!"

But Jesus, knowing their thoughts, said, "Why do you think evil in your hearts? For which is easier, to say, 'Your sins are forgiven you,' or to say, 'Arise and walk'? But that you may know that the Son of Man has power on earth to forgive sins"—then He said to the paralytic, "Arise, take up your bed, and go to your house." And he arose and departed to his house.

Matthew 9:2-7 NKJV

While he was saying these thing to them an official came up to him and, bowing low before him, said, "My daughter has just this moment died. Please come and lay your hand on her and she will come back to life!"

At this Jesus got to his feet and followed him, accompanied by his disciples. And on the way a woman who had a haemorrhage for twelve years approached him from behind and touched the edge of his cloak.

"If I can only touch his cloak," she kept saying to herself, "I shall be all right."

But Jesus turned right round and saw her. "Cheer up, my daughter," he said, "your faith has made you well!" And the woman was completely cured from that moment.

Then when Jesus came into the official's house and noticed the flute-players and the noisy crowd he said, "You must all go outside; the little girl is not dead, she is fast asleep."

This was met with scornful laughter. But when Jesus had forced the crowd to leave, he came right into the room, took hold of her hand, and the girl got up. And this became the talk of the whole district.

Matthew 9:18-25 Phillips

As Jesus went on from there, two blind men followed him, calling out, "Have mercy on us, Son of David!"

When he had gone indoors, the blind men came to him, and he asked them, "Do you believe that I am able to do this?"

"Yes, Lord," they replied.

Then he touched their eyes and said, "According to your faith let it be done to you"; and their sight was restored. Jesus warned them sternly, "See that no one knows about this." But they went out and spread the news about him all over that region.

Matthew 9:27-31 NIV

After sending them home, he went up into the hills by himself to pray. Night fell while he was there alone.

Meanwhile, the disciples were in trouble far away from land, for a strong wind had risen, and they were fighting heavy waves. About three o'clock in the morning Jesus came toward them, walking on the water. When the disciples saw him walking on the water, they were terrified. In their fear, they cried out, "It's a ghost!"

But Jesus spoke to them at once. "Don't be afraid," he said. "Take courage. I am here!"

Then Peter called to him, "Lord, if it's really you, tell me to come to you, walking on the water."

"Yes, come," Jesus said.

So Peter went over the side of the boat and walked on the water toward Jesus. But when he saw the strong wind and the waves, he was terrified and began to sink. "Save me, Lord!" he shouted.

Jesus immediately reached out and grabbed him. "You have so little faith," Jesus said. "Why did you doubt me?"

When they climbed back into the boat, the wind stopped. Then the disciples worshiped him. "You really are the Son of God!" they exclaimed.

Matthew 14:23-33 NLT

When Jesus and his followers came back to the crowd, a man came to Jesus and bowed before him. The man said, "Lord, have mercy on my son. He has epilepsy and is suffering very much, because he often falls into the fire or into the water. I brought him to your followers, but they could not cure him."

Jesus answered, "You people have no faith, and your lives are all wrong. How long must I put up with you? How long must I continue to be patient with you? Bring the boy here." Jesus commanded the demon inside the boy. Then the demon came out, and the boy was healed from that time on.

The followers came to Jesus when he was alone and asked, "Why couldn't we force the demon out?"

Jesus answered, "Because your faith is too small. I tell you the truth, if your faith is as big as a mustard seed, you can say to this mountain, 'Move from here to there,' and it will move. All things will be possible for you.

Matthew 17:14-20 NCV

With God all things are possible.

Matthew 19:26

Jesus looked at them and said, "For people this is impossible, but for God all things are possible."

Matthew 19:26 NCV

And Jesus answered them, Truly I say to you, if you have faith (a firm relying trust) and do not doubt, you will not only do what has been done to the fig tree, but even if you say to this mountain, Be taken up and cast into the sea, it will be done.

And whatever you ask for in prayer, having faith and (really) believing, you will receive.

Matthew 21:21,22 AMP

Heaven and earth will pass away, but my words will never pass away.

Matthew 24:35 AMP

And he said unto them, Take heed what ye hear: with what measure ye mete, it shall be measured to you: and unto you that hear shall more be given.

For he that hath, to him shall be given: and he that hath not, from him shall be taken even that which he hath.

And he said, So is the kingdom of God, as if a man should cast seed into the ground;

And should sleep, and rise night and day, and the seed should spring and grow up, he knoweth not how.

For the earth bringeth forth fruit of herself; first the blade, then the ear, after that the full corn in the ear.

But when the fruit is brought forth, immediately he putteth in the sickle, because the harvest is come.

And he said, Whereunto shall we liken the kingdom of God? or with what comparison shall we compare it?

It is like a grain of mustard seed, which, when it is sown in the earth, is less than all the seeds that be in the earth:

But when it is sown, it groweth up, and becometh greater than all herbs, and shooteth out great branches; so that the fowls of the air may lodge under the shadow of it.

Mark 4:24-32

Jesus looked straight at them and said, "Humanly speaking it is impossible, but not with God. Everything is possible with God."

Mark 10:27 Phillips

Jesus said, 'What do you want me to do for you?' The blind man said to him, 'Teacher I want to see.' Jesus said, 'Go home. Because you believe in me, your faith has made you well.' Right then he was able to see. He followed Jesus on the road.

Mark 10:51-52 WE

Then Jesus said to the disciples, "Have faith in God. I tell you the truth, you can say to this mountain, 'May you be lifted up and thrown into the sea' and it will happen. But you must really believe it will happen and have no doubt in your heart. I tell you, you can pray for anything, and if you believe that you've received it, it will be yours. But when you are praying, first forgive anyone you are holding a grudge against, so that your Father in heaven will forgive your sins, too."

Mark 11:22-26 NLT

For no promise of God can fail to be fulfilled.

Luke 1:37 Phillips

For with God nothing is ever impossible and no word from God shall be without power or impossible of fulfillment.

Luke 1:37 AMP

You are blessed because you believed that the Lord would do what he said.

Luke 1:45 NLT

Then He said to her, "Your sins are forgiven."

And those who sat at the table with Him began to say to themselves, "Who is this who even forgives sins?"

Then He said to the woman, "Your faith has saved you. Go in peace."

Luke 7:48-50 NKJV

His disciples asked him what this parable meant. He said, "The knowledge of the secrets of the kingdom of God has been given to you, but to others I speak in parables, so that, "'though seeing, they may not see; though hearing, they may not understand.'

"This is the meaning of the parable: The seed is the word of God. Those along the path are the ones who hear, and then the devil comes and takes away the word from their hearts, so that they may not believe and be saved. Those on the rocky ground are the ones who receive the word with joy when they hear it, but they have no root. They believe for a while, but in the time of testing they fall away. The seed that fell among thorns stands for those who hear, but as they go on their way they are choked by life's worries, riches and pleasures, and they do not mature. But the seed on good soil stands for those with a noble and good heart, who hear the word, retain it, and by persevering produce a crop.

Luke 8:9-15 NIV

And so I tell you, keep on asking, and you will receive what you ask for. Keep on seeking, and you will find. Keep on knocking, and the door will be opened to you. For everyone who asks, receives. Everyone who seeks, finds. And to everyone who knocks, the door will be opened.

Luke 11:9-10 NLT

If you are faithful in little things, you will be faithful in large ones.

Luke 16:10 NLT

The apostles said to the Lord, "Give us more faith!"

The Lord said, "If your faith were the size of a mustard seed, you could say to this mulberry tree, 'Dig yourself up and plant yourself in the sea,' and it would obey you.

Luke 17:5-6 NCV

Now it happened as He went to Jerusalem that He passed through the midst of Samaria and Galilee. Then as He entered a certain village, there met Him ten men who were lepers, who stood afar off. And they lifted up their voices and said, "Jesus, Master, have mercy on us!"

So when He saw them, He said to them, "Go, show yourselves to the priests." And so it was that as they went, they were cleansed.

And one of them, when he saw that he was healed, returned, and with a loud voice glorified God, and fell down on his face at His feet, giving Him thanks. And he was a Samaritan.

So Jesus answered and said, "Were there not ten cleansed? But where are the nine? Were there not any found who returned to give glory to God except this foreigner?" And He said to him, "Arise, go your way. Your faith has made you well."

Luke 17:11-19 NKJV

Jesus replied, "What men find impossible is perfectly possible with God."

Luke 18:27 Phillips

He said, "Master, I want to see you again."

Jesus said, "Go ahead – see again! Your faith has saved and healed you!" The healing was instant: He looked up, seeing and then followed Jesus, glorifying God. Everyone in the street joined in, shouting praise to God.

Luke 18:41-43 MSG

Oh Simon, Simon, do you know that Satan has asked to have you all to sift like wheat? – but I have prayed for you that you may not lose your faith. Yes, when you have turned back to me, you must strengthen these brothers of yours."

Luke 22:31-32 Phillips

But to all who believed and accepted him, he gave the right to become children of God.

John 1:12 NLT

God loved the world so much that he gave his one and only Son so that whoever believes in him may not be lost, but have eternal life. God did not send his Son into the world to judge the world guilty, but to save the world through him.

John 3:16-17 NCV

Now a certain man was there who had an infirmity thirty-eight years.

When Jesus saw him lying there, and knew that he already had been in that condition a long time, He said to him, "Do you want to be made well?"

The sick man answered Him, "Sir, I have no man to put me into the pool when the water is stirred up; but while I am coming, another steps down before me."

Jesus said to him, "Rise, take up your bed and walk." And immediately the man was made well, took up his bed, and walked.

And that day was the Sabbath.

John 5:5-9 NKJV

The work of God is this: to believe in the one he has sent.

John 6:29 NIV

He who believes in Me (who cleanses to and trust in and relies on me) as the Scripture has said, From his innermost be-ing shall flow (continuously) springs and rivers of living water.

John 7:38 AMP

`Do you believe in the Son of God?'

He answered, `Sir, who is the Son of God? Tell me, so that I may believe in him.'

Jesus said, `You have already seen him. The person who is

talking to you now, he is the Son of God.'

The man said, `Sir, I do believe.' He kneeled down in front of Jesus and worshipped him.

John 9:35-38 WE

Do not believe me unless I do the works of my Father.

But if I do them, even though you do not believe me, believe the works, that you may know and understand that the Father is in me, and I in the Father.

John 10:37-38 NIV

Roll the stone aside," Jesus told them.

But Martha, the dead man's sister, protested, "Lord, he has been dead for four days. The smell will be terrible."

Jesus responded, "Didn't I tell you that you would see God's glory if you believe?" So they rolled the stone aside. Then Jesus looked up to heaven and said, "Father, thank you for hearing me. You always hear me, but I said it out loud for the sake of all these

people standing here, so that they will believe you sent me." Then Jesus shouted, "Lazarus, come out!" And the dead man came out, his hands and feet bound in graveclothes, his face wrapped in a headcloth. Jesus told them, "Unwrap him and let him go!"

Many of the people who were with Mary believed in Jesus when they saw this happen.

John 11:39-45 NLT

Don't you believe that I am in the Father, and that the Father is in me? The words I say to you I do not speak on my own authority. Rather, it is the Father, living in me, who is doing his work. Believe me when I say that I am in the Father and the Father is in me; or at least believe on the evidence of the works themselves. Very truly I tell you, whoever believes in me will do the works I have been doing, and they will do even greater things than these, because I am going to the Father. And I will do whatever you ask in my name, so that the Father may be glorified in the Son. You may ask me for anything in my name, and I will do it.

John 14:10-14 NIV

Now Thomas, called the Twin, one of the twelve, was not with them when Jesus came. The other disciples therefore said to him, "We have seen the Lord."

So he said to them, "Unless I see in His hands the print of the nails, and put my finger into the print of the nails, and put my hand into His side, I will not believe."

And after eight days His disciples were again inside, and Thomas with them. Jesus came, the doors being shut, and stood in the midst, and said, "Peace to you!" Then He said to Thomas, "Reach your finger here, and look at My hands; and reach your hand here, and put it into My side. Do not be unbelieving, but believing."

And Thomas answered and said to Him, "My Lord and my God!"

Jesus said to him, "Thomas, because you have seen Me, you have believed. Blessed are those who have not seen and yet have believed."

And truly Jesus did many other signs in the presence of His disciples, which are not written in this book;

John 20:24-30 NKJV

Peter and John went to the Temple one afternoon to take part in the three o'clock prayer service. As they approached the Temple, a man lame from birth was being carried in. Each day he was put beside the Temple gate, the one called the Beautiful Gate, so he could beg from the people going into the Temple. When he saw Peter and John about to enter, he asked them for some money.

Peter and John looked at him intently, and Peter said, "Look at us!" The lame man looked at them eagerly, expecting some money. But Peter said, "I don't have any silver or gold for you. But I'll give you what I have. In the name of Jesus Christ the Nazarene, get up and walk!"

Then Peter took the lame man by the right hand and helped him up. And as he did, the man's feet and ankles were instantly healed and strengthened. He jumped up, stood on his feet, and began to walk! Then, walking, leaping, and praising God, he went into the Temple with them.

Through faith in the name of Jesus, this man was healed— and you know how crippled he was before. Faith in Jesus' name has healed him before your very eyes.

Acts 3:1-8, 16 NLT

But many of the people who heard them speak the word of God, believed what they said. The number of men who believed was about five thousand.

Acts 4:4 WE

And Stephen, full of faith and power, did great wonders and miracles among the people.

Acts 6:8 NCV

Therefore take heart, men, for I believe God that it will be just as it was told me.

Acts 27:25 NKJV

So keep up your courage, men, for I have faith (complete confidence) in God that it will be exactly as it was told me.

Acts 27:25 AMP

First I want to say that I thank my God through Jesus Christ for all of you, because people everywhere in the world are talking about your faith.

Romans 1:8 NCV

For I am not ashamed of the gospel of Christ: for it is the power of God unto salvation to everyone that believeth; to the Jew first, and also to the Greek.

For therein is the righteousness of God revealed from faith to faith: as it is written, The just shall live by faith.

Romans 1:16,17 NIV

True, some of them were unfaithful; but just because they were unfaithful, does that mean God will be unfaithful? Of course not! Even if everyone else is a liar, God is true. As the Scriptures say about him,

"You will be proved right in what you say, and you will win your case in court."

Romans 3:3-4 NLT

Therefore by the deeds of the law there shall no flesh be justified in his sight: for by the law is the knowledge of sin.

But now the righteousness of God without the law is manifested, being witnessed by the law and the prophets;

Even the righteousness of God which is by faith of Jesus Christ unto all and upon all them that believe: for there is no difference:

For all have sinned, and come short of the glory of God;

Being justified freely by his grace through the redemption that is in Christ Jesus:

Whom God hath set forth to be a propitiation through faith in his blood, to declare his righteousness for the remission of sins that are past, through the forbearance of God;

To declare, I say, at this time his righteousness: that he might be just, and the justifier of him which believeth in Jesus.

Where is boasting then? It is excluded. By what law? of works? Nay: but by the law of faith.

Therefore we conclude that a man is justified by faith without the deeds of the law.

Is he the God of the Jews only? is he not also of the Gentiles? Yes, of the Gentiles also:

Seeing it is one God, which shall justify the circumcision by faith, and uncircumcision through faith.

Do we then make void the law through faith? God forbid: yea, we establish the law.

Romans 3:20-31 KJV

So how do we fit what we know of Abraham, our first father in the faith, into this new way of looking at things? If Abraham, by what he did for God, got God to approve him, he could certainly have taken credit for it. But the story we're given is a God-story, not an Abraham-story. What we read in Scripture is, "Abraham entered into what God was doing for him, and that was the turning point. He trusted God to set him right instead of trying to be right on his own."

If you're a hard worker and do a good job, you deserve your pay; we don't call your wages a gift. But if you see that the job is too big for you, that it's something only God can do, and you trust him to do it—you could never do it for yourself no matter how hard and long you worked—well, that trusting him to do it is what gets you set right with God, by God. Sheer gift.

Romans 4:1-5 MSG

We have been saying that Abraham's faith was credited to him as righteousness. Under what circumstances was it credited? Was it after he was circumcised, or before? It was not after, but before!

And he received circumcision as a sign, a seal of the righteousness that he had by faith while he was still uncircumcised. So then, he is the father of all who believe but have not been circumcised, in order that righteousness might be credited to them. And he is then also the father of the circumcised who not only are circumcised but who also follow in the footsteps of the faith that our father Abraham had before he was circumcised.

It was not through the law that Abraham and his offspring received the promise that he would be heir of the world, but through the righteousness that comes by faith. For if those who depend on the law are heirs, faith means nothing and the promise is worthless, because the law brings wrath. And where there is no law there is no transgression.

Therefore, the promise comes by faith, so that it may be by grace and may be guaranteed to all Abraham's offspring—not only to those who are of the law but also to those who have the faith of Abraham. He is the father of us all. As it is written: "I have made you a father of many nations." He is our father in the sight of God, in whom he believed—the God who gives life to the dead and calls into being things that were not.

Against all hope, Abraham in hope believed and so became the father of many nations, just as it had been said to him, "So shall your offspring be." Without weakening in his faith, he faced the fact that his body was as good as dead—since he was about a hundred years old—and that Sarah's womb was also dead. Yet he did not waver through unbelief regarding the promise of God, but was strengthened in his faith and gave glory to God, being fully persuaded that God had power to do what he had promised. This is why "it was credited to him as righteousness." The words "it was credited to him" were written not for him alone, but also for us, to whom God will credit righteousness—for us who believe in him who raised Jesus our Lord from the dead. He was delivered over to death for our sins and was raised to life for our justification.

Romans 4:9-25 NIV

Therefore, since we have been made right in God's sight by faith, we have peace with God because of what Jesus Christ our Lord has done for us. Because of our faith, Christ has brought us into this place of undeserved privilege where we now stand, and we confidently and joyfully look forward to sharing God's glory.

Romans 5:1-2 NLT

We are made good people and put right with God when we believe in Jesus Christ. So now we have peace with God because of what our Lord Jesus Christ did.

Because we believe, Christ has brought us to the place where God can do us good. We are in that place now. We are very happy because we have the hope that we shall see God's greatness.

Romans 5:1-2 WE

So now, those who are in Christ Jesus are not judged guilty.

Romans 8:1 NCV

So now there is no condemnation for those who belong to Christ Jesus.

Romans 8:1 NLT

But if the Spirit of him that raised up Jesus from the dead dwell in you, he that raised up Christ from the dead shall also quicken your mortal bodies by His Spirit that dwelleth in you.

Romans 8:11 KJV

If God be for us, who can be against us?

Romans 8:31

What then shall we say? That the Gentiles, who did not pursue righteousness, have obtained it, a righteousness that is by faith; but the people of Israel, who pursued the law as the way of righteousness, have not attained their goal. Why not? Because they pursued it not by faith but as if it were by works. They stumbled over the stumbling stone. As it is written:

"See, I lay in Zion a stone that causes people to stumble and a rock that makes them fall, and the one who believes in him will never be put to shame."

Romans 9:30-33 NIV

But faith's way of getting right with God says, "Don't say in your heart, 'Who will go up to heaven?' (to bring Christ down to earth). And don't say, 'Who will go down to the place of the dead?' (to bring Christ back to life again)." In fact, it says, "The message is very close at hand; it is on your lips and in your heart."

And that message is the very message about faith that we preach: If you confess with your mouth that Jesus is Lord and believe in your heart that God raised him from the dead, you will be saved. For it is by believing in your heart that you are made right with God, and it is by confessing with your mouth that you are

saved. As the Scriptures tell us, "Anyone who trusts in him will never be disgraced." Jew and Gentile are the same in this respect. They have the same Lord, who gives generously to all who call on him. For "Everyone who calls on the name of the LORD will be saved."

But how can they call on him to save them unless they believe in him? And how can they believe in him if they have never heard about him? And how can they hear about him unless someone tells them? And how will anyone go and tell them without being sent? That is why the Scriptures say, "How beautiful are the feet of messengers who bring good news!"

But not everyone welcomes the Good News, for Isaiah the prophet said, "LORD, who has believed our message?" So faith comes from hearing, that is, hearing the Good News about Christ.

Romans 10:6-17 NLT

If the first piece of bread is holy, so is all the rest which came from the same bread mix. If the root of a tree is holy, the branches are holy also.

Maybe some of the tree's branches were broken off. And you, a branch from a wild olive tree, were made to grow on the tree among the branches. You then have the good water that comes from the root of the olive tree.

But do not think that you are better than the tree's own branches. If you do, remember it is not you that holds the root in place. But it is the root that holds you.

Then you will say, `The branches were broken off so that I might be joined to the tree.'

That is true. They were broken off because they did not believe. And you have your place only because you believe. So do not be proud, but fear.

If God punished the tree's own branches, he will punish you also.

See how kind God is. And see how hard he is. He is hard

on those who have fallen. But God is kind to you if you go on follow-

ing in his ways. If you do not, you also will be broken off.

God will also put back the other branches if they believe. God is able to put the Jews back where they belong.

Romans 11:16-23 WE

You are what you are because God has given you something when you believed.

Romans 12:3 WE

I am convinced, and I say this as in the presence of Christ himself, that nothing is intrinsically unholy. But none the less it is unholy to the man who thinks it is. If your habit of unrestricted diet seriously upsets your brother, you are no longer living in love towards him. And surely you wouldn't let food mean ruin to a man for whom Christ died. You mustn't let something that is all right for you look like an evil practice to somebody else. After all, the kingdom of Heaven is not a matter of whether you get what you like to eat and drink, but of righteousness and peace and joy in the Holy Spirit. If you put these things first in serving Christ you will please God and are not likely to offend men. So let us concentrate on the things which make for harmony, and on the growth of one another's character. Surely we shouldn't wish to undo God's work for the sake of a plate of meat!

I freely admit that all food is, in itself. harmless, but it can be harmful to the man who eats it with a guilty conscience. We should be willing to be both vegetarians and teetotallers if by doing otherwise we should impede a brother's progress in faith. Your personal convictions are a matter of faith between yourself and God, and you are happy if you have no qualms about what you allow yourself to eat. Yet if a man eats meat with an uneasy conscience about it, you may be sure he is wrong to do so. For his action does not spring from his faith, and when we act apart from our faith we sin.

Romans 14:22-23 Phillips

Now the God of hope fill you with all joy in peace in believing, that ye may abound in hope, through the power of the Holy Ghost.

Romans 15:13 KJV

God gives hope. May he make you very happy. May he give you peace because you believe. Then the power of the Holy Spirit will give you much hope.

Romans 15:13 WE

God, who got you started in this spiritual adventure, shares with us the life of his Son and our Master Jesus. He will never give up o you. Never forget that.

I Corinthians 1:9 MSG

For since in the wisdom of God the world through its wisdom did not know him, God was pleased through the foolishness of what was preached to save those who believe. Jews demand signs
and Greeks look for wisdom, but we preach Christ crucified: a stumbling block to Jews and foolishness to Gentiles, but to those whom God has called, both Jews and Greeks, Christ the power of God and the wisdom of God. For the foolishness of God is wiser than human wisdom, and the weakness of God is stronger than human strength.

Brothers and sisters, think of what you were when you were called. Not many of you were wise by human standards; not many were influential; not many were of noble birth. But God chose the foolish things of the world to shame the wise; God chose the weak things of the world to shame the strong. God chose the lowly things of this world and the despised things— and the things that are not—to nullify the things that are, so that no one may boast before him. It is because of him that you are in Christ Jesus, who has become for us wisdom from God— that is, our righteousness, holiness and redemption. Therefore, as it is written: "Let the one who boasts boast in the Lord."

I Corinthians 1:21-31 NIV

And my message and my preaching were very plain. Rather than using clever and persuasive speeches, I relied only on the power of the Holy Spirit. I did this so you would trust not in human wisdom but in the power of God.

I Corinthians 2:4-5 NLT

Something from the Spirit can be seen in each person, for the common good. The Spirit gives one person the ability to speak with wisdom, and the same Spirit gives another the ability to speak with knowledge. The same Spirit gives faith to one person. And, to another, that one Spirit gives gifts of healing. The Spirit gives to another person the power to do miracles, to another the ability to prophesy. And he gives to another the ability to know the difference between good and evil spirits. The Spirit gives one person the ability to speak in different kinds of languages and to

another the ability to interpret those languages. One Spirit, the same Spirit, does all these things, and the Spirit decides what to give each person.

I Corinthians 12:7-11 NCV

If I have the gift of prophecy and can fathom all mysteries and all knowledge, and if I have a faith that can move mountains, but do not have love, I am nothing.

I Corinthians 13:2 NIV

Watch, stand fast in the faith, be brave, be strong. Let all that you do be done with love.

I Corinthians 16:13-14 NKJV

For all the promises of God in him are yea, and in him Amen, unto the glory of God by us.

2 Corinthians 1:20

We are not trying to control your faith. You are strong in faith. But we are workers with you for your own joy.

2 Corinthians 1:24 NCV

We have the same faithful spirit as what is written in scripture: I had faith, and so I spoke. We also have faith, and so we also speak.

2 Corinthians 4:13 CEB

Therefore we do not lose heart. Though outwardly we are wasting away, yet inwardly we are being renewed day by day. For our light and momentary troubles are achieving for us an eternal glory that far outweighs them all. So we fix our eyes not on what is seen, but on what is unseen, since what is seen is temporary, but what is unseen is eternal.

2 Corinthians 4:16-18 NIV

For we walk by faith, not by sight.

2 Corinthians 5:7

For we live by believing and not by seeing.

2 Corinthians 5:7 NLT

But since you excel in everything – in faith, in speech, in knowledge, in complete earnestness and in the love we have kindled in you – see that you also excel in this grace of giving.

2 Corinthians 8:7 NIV

The truth is that, although we lead normal human lives, the battle we are fighting is on the spiritual level.

The very weapons we use are not human but powerful in God's warfare for the destruction of the enemy's strongholds.

Our battle is to break down every deceptive argument and every imposing defence that men erect against the true knowledge of God. We fight to capture every thought until it acknowledges the authority of Christ.

2 Corinthians 10:3-5 Phillips

Examine yourselves as to whether you are in the faith. Test yourselves. Do you not know yourselves, that Jesus Christ is in you? – unless indeed you are disqualified.

But I trust that you will know that we are not disqualified.

2 Corinthians 13:5-6 NKJV

Yet we know that a person is made right with God not by following the law, but by trusting in Jesus Christ. So we, too, have put our faith in Christ Jesus, that we might be made right with God because we trusted in Christ. It is not because we followed the law, because no one can be made right with God by following the law.

Galatians 2:16 NCV

I am crucified with Christ nevertheless I live; yet not I, but Christ liveth in me: and the life which I now live in the flesh I live by the faith of the Son of God, who loved me, and gave himself for me.

Galatians 2:20

You foolish Galatians! Who has bewitched you? Before your very eyes Jesus Christ was clearly portrayed as crucified. I would like to learn just one thing from you: Did you receive the Spirit by the works of the law, or by believing what you heard? Are you so foolish? After beginning by means of the Spirit, are you now trying to finish by means of the flesh? Have you experienced so much in vain—if it really was in vain? So again I ask, does God give you his Spirit and work miracles among you by the works of the law, or by your believing what you heard? So also Abraham "believed God, and it was credited to him as righteousness."

Understand, then, that those who have faith are children of Abraham. Scripture foresaw that God would justify the Gentiles by faith, and announced the gospel in advance to Abraham: "All nations will be blessed through you." So those who rely on faith are blessed along with Abraham, the man of faith.

For all who rely on the works of the law are under a curse, as it is written: "Cursed is everyone who does not continue to do everything written in the Book of the Law." Clearly no one who relies on the law is justified before God, because "the righteous will live by faith." The law is not based on faith; on the contrary, it says, "The person who does these things will live by them." Christ redeemed us from the curse of the law by becoming a curse for us, for it is written: "Cursed is everyone who is hung on a pole." He redeemed us in order that the blessing given to Abraham might come to the Gentiles through Christ Jesus, so that by faith we might receive the promise of the Spirit.

Galatians 3:1-14 NIV

But the Scriptures declare that we are all prisoners of sin, so we receive God's promise of freedom only by believing in

Jesus Christ.

Before the way of faith in Christ was unavailable to us, we were placed under guard by the law. We were kept in protective custody, so to speak, until the way of faith was revealed.

Let me put it another way. The law was our guardian until Christ came; it protected us until we could be made right with God through faith. And now that the way of faith has come, we no longer need the law as our guardian.

For you are all children of God through faith in Christ Jesus.

Galatians 3:22-26 NLT

The only thing that counts is faith expressing itself through love.

Galatians 5:6 NIV

I also pray that you will understand the incredible greatness of God's power for us who believe him. This is the same mighty power that raised Christ from the dead and seated him in the place of honor at God's right hand in the heavenly realm. Now he is far above any ruler or authority or power or leader or anything else – not only in this world but also in the world to come. God has put all things under the authority of Christ and has made him head over all things for the benefit of the church.

And the church is his body; it is made full and complete by Christ, who fills all things everywhere with himself.

Ephesians 1:19-23 NLT

For it is by free grace (God's unmerited favor) that you are saved (delivered from judgment and made partakers of Christ's salvation) through your faith. And this (salvation) is not of yourselves (of your own doing, it came not through your own striving), but it is the gift of God.

Ephesians 2:8 AMP

In Christ we can come before God with freedom and without fear. We can do this through faith in Christ.

Ephesians 3:12 NCV

It is in this same Jesus, because we have faith in him, that we dare, even with confidence, to approach God.

Ephesians 3:12 Phillips

Finally, be strong in the Lord and in his mighty power. Put on the full armor of God, so that you can take your stand against the devil's schemes. For our struggle is not against flesh and blood, but against the rulers, against the authorities, against the powers of this dark world and against the spiritual forces of evil in the heavenly realms. Therefore put on the full armor of God, so that when the day of evil comes, you may be able to stand your ground, and after you have done everything, to stand. Stand firm then, with the belt of truth buckled around your waist, with the breastplate of righteousness in place, and with your feet fitted with the readiness that comes from the gospel of peace. In addition to all this, take up the shield of faith, with which you can extinguish all the flaming arrows of the evil one. Take the helmet

of salvation and the sword of the Spirit, which is the word of God.

And pray in the Spirit on all occasions with all kinds of prayers and requests. With this in mind, be alert and always keep on praying for all the Lord's people.

Ephesians 6:10-18 NIV

Not only those things, but I think that all things are worth nothing compared with the greatness of knowing Christ Jesus my Lord. Because of him, I have lost all those things, and now I know they are worthless trash. This allows me to have Christ and to belong to him. Now I am right with God, not because I followed the law, but because I believed in Christ. God uses my faith to make me right with him. I want to know Christ and the power that raised him from the dead. I want to share in his sufferings and become like him in his death.

Philippians 3:8-10 NCV

Once you were alienated from God and were enemies in your minds because of your evil behavior. But now he has reconciled you by Christ's physical body through death to present you holy in his sight, without blemish and free from accusation – if you

continue in your faith, established and firm, and do not move from the hope held out in the gospel. This is the gospel that you heard and that has been proclaimed to every creature under

heaven, and of which I, Paul have become a servant.

Colossians 1:21-23 NIV

But let us who live in the light be clearheaded, protected by the armor of faith and love, and wearing as our helmet the confidence of our salvation.

I Thessalonians 5:8 NLT

My brothers, we thank God for you always. It is the right thing to do. You trust him more and more. You all love each other more and more.

So we are proud of you. We tell the churches of God about you because you are standing strong and you keep on believing in God. Your troubles and hard times do not stop you.

2 Thessalonians 1:3-4 WE

In view of this great prospect, we pray for you constantly, that God will think you worthy of this calling, and that he will effect in you all his goodness desires to do, and that your faith makes possible. We pray that the name of our Lord Jesus Christ may become more glorious through you, and that you may share something of his glory – all through the grace of our God and Jesus Christ the Lord.

2 Thessalonians 1:11-12 Phillips

The grace of our Lord was poured out on me abundantly, along with the faith and love that are in Christ Jesus.

I Timothy 1:14 NIV

Timothy, my son, here are my instructions for you, based on the prophetic words spoken about you earlier. May they help you fight well in the Lord's battles. Cling to your faith in Christ, and keep your conscience clear. For some people have deliberately violated their consciences; as a result, their faith has been shipwrecked.

I Timothy 1:18-19 NLT

In the same way, the leaders helpers must be men whom people respect. They must not say one thing one time and something different another time. They must not drink too much wine. They must not try to get rich in wrong ways.

They must know God's plan and what we believe. They must do only what they know is right.

I Timothy 3:8-9 WE

Let no one despise your youth, but be an example to the believers in word, in conduct, in love, in spirit, in faith, in purity. Till I come, give attention to reading, to exhortation, to doctrine. Do not neglect the gift that is in you, which was given to you by prophecy with the laying on of the hands of the eldership. Meditate on these things; give yourself entirely to them, that your progress may be evident to all. Take heed to yourself and to the doctrine. Continue in them, for in doing this you will save both yourself and those who hear you.

I Timothy 4:12-16 NKJV

But thou, O man of God, flee these things; and follow after righteousness, godliness, faith, love, patience, meekness.

Fight the good fight of faith, lay hold on eternal life, whereunto thou art also called, and hast professed a good profession before many witnesses.

I Timothy 6:11-12

That is why I am suffering here in prison. But I am not ashamed of it, for I know the one in whom I trust, and I am sure that he is able to guard what I have entrusted to him until the day of his return.

Hold on to the pattern of wholesome teaching you learned from me—a pattern shaped by the faith and love that you have in Christ Jesus. Through the power of the Holy Spirit who lives within us, carefully guard the precious truth that has been entrusted to you.

2 Timothy 1:12-14 NLT

This teaching is true:

If we died with him, we will also live with him.

If we accept suffering, we will also rule with him.

If we say we don't know him, he will say he doesn't know us.

If we are not faithful, he will still be faithful,

Because he must be true to who he is.

2 Timothy 2:11-13 NCV

Flee the evil desires of you and pursue righteousness, faith, love

and peace, along with those who call on the Lord out of a pure heart.

2 Timothy 2:2 NIV

I have fought the good fight, I have finished the race, I have kept the faith.

2 Timothy 4:7 NCV

I have fought the good fight, I have finished the race, I have kept the faith. Finally, there is laid up for me the crown of righteousness, which the Lord, the righteous Judge, will give to me on that Day, and not to me only but also to all who have loved His appearing.

2 Timothy 4:7-8 NKJV

I always thank my God as I remember you in my prayers, be cause I hear about your love for all his holy people and your faith in the Lord Jesus. I pray that your partnership with us in the faith may be effective in deepening your understanding of every good thing we share for the sake of Christ.

Philemon 4-6 NIV

Therefore, while the promise of entering His rest still holds and is offered [today], let us be afraid [to distrust it], lest any of you should think he has come too late and has come short of [reaching] it.

For indeed we have had the glad tidings [Gospel of God] proclaimed to us just as truly as they [the Israelites of old did when the good news of deliverance from bondage came to them]; but the message they heard did not benefit them, because it was not mixed with faith (with the leaning of the entire personality on God in absolute trust and confidence in His power, wisdom, and goodness) by those who heard it; neither were they united in faith with the ones [Joshua and Caleb] who heard (did believe).

For we who have believed (adhered to and trusted in and relied on God) do enter that rest, in accordance with His declaration that those [who did not believe] should not enter when

He said, As I swore in My wrath, They shall not enter My rest;
and this He said although [His] works had been completed and
prepared
[and waiting for all who would believe] from the foundation of
the world.

Hebrews 4:1-3 AMP

So let us stop going over the basic teachings about Christ
again and again. Let us go on instead and become mature in
our understanding. Surely we don't need to start again with the
fundamen
tal importance of repenting from evil deeds and placing our
faith in God.

Hebrews 6:1 NLT

Let us come near to God with a sincere heart and a sure faith,
because we have been made free from a guilty conscience,
and our bodies have been washed with pure water. Let us hold
firmly to the hope that we have confessed, because we can trust
God to do what he promised.

Hebrews 10:22-23 NCV

Let us do all we can to help one another's faith, and this the more earnestly as we see the final day drawing every nearer.

Hebrews 10:25 Phillips

And my righteous one will live by faith. But I will take no pleasure in anyone who turns away.

But we are not like those who turn away from God to their own destruction. We are the faithful ones, whose souls will be saved.

Hebrews 10:38-39 NLT

Faith is the confidence that what we hope for will actually happen; it gives us assurance about things we cannot see. Through their faith, the people in days of old earned a good reputation.

By faith, we can understand that the entire universe was formed at God's command, that what we now see did not come from anything that can be seen.

It was by faith that Abel brought a more acceptable offering to God than Cain did. Abel's offering gave evidence that he was a righteous man, and God showed his approval of his gifts. Although Abel is long dead, he still speaks to us by his example of faith.

It was by faith that Enoch was taken up to heaven without dying – "he disappeared, because God took him." For before he was taken up, he was known as a person who pleased God. And it is impossible to please God without faith. Anyone who wants to come to him must believe that God exists and that he rewards those who sincerely seek him.

Hebrews 11:1-6 NLT

It was by faith that Noah built a large boat to save his family from the flood. He obeyed God, who warned him about things that had never happened before. By his faith, Noah condemned the rest of the world, and he received the righteousness that comes by faith.

It was by faith that Abraham obeyed when God called him to leave home and go to another land that God would give him as his inheritance. He went without knowing where he was going. And even when he reached the land God promised him, he lived there by faith – for he was like a foreigner, living in tents. And so did Isaac and Jacob, who inherited the same promise. Abraham was confidently looking forward to a city with eternal foundations, a city designed and built by God.

It was by faith that even Sarah was able to have a child,

though she was barren and was too old. She believed that God would keep his promise. And so a whole nation came from this one man who was as good as dead – a nation with so many people that, like the stars in the sky and the sand on the seashore, there is no way to count them.

All these people died still believing what God had promised them. They did not receive what was promised, but they saw it all from a distance and welcomed it. They agreed that they were foreigners and nomads here on earth.

Hebrews 11:7-13 NLT

By faith Abraham, when God tested him, offered Isaac as a sacrifice. He who had embraced the promises was about to sacrifice his one and only son, even though God had said to him, "It is through Isaac that your offspring will be reckoned." Abraham reasoned that God could even raise the dead, and so in a manner of speaking he did receive Isaac back from death.

By faith Isaac blessed Jacob and Esau in regard to their future.

By faith Jacob, when he was dying, blessed each of Joseph's sons, and worshiped as he leaned on the top of his staff.

By faith Joseph, when his end was near, spoke about the exodus of the Israelites from Egypt and gave instructions concerning the burial of his bones.

By faith Moses' parents hid him for three months after he was born, because they saw he was no ordinary child, and they were not afraid of the king's edict.

By faith Moses, when he had grown up, refused to be known as the son of Pharaoh's daughter. He chose to be mistreated along with the people of God rather than to enjoy the fleeting pleasures

of sin. He regarded disgrace for the sake of Christ as of greater value than the treasures of Egypt, because he was looking ahead to his reward. By faith he left Egypt, not fearing the king's anger; he persevered because he saw him who is invisible. By faith he kept the Passover and the application of blood, so that the destroyer of the firstborn would not touch the firstborn of Israel.

By faith the people passed through the Red Sea as on dry land; but when the Egyptians tried to do so, they were drowned.

By faith the walls of Jericho fell, after the army had marched around them for seven days.

By faith the prostitute Rahab, because she welcomed the spies, was not killed with those who were disobedient

Hebrews 11:17-31 NIV

We are surrounded by a great cloud of people whose lives tell us what faith means. So let us run the race that is before us and never give up. We should remove from our lives anything that would get in the way and the sin that so easily holds us back. Let us look only to Jesus, the One who began our faith and who makes it perfect. He suffered death on the cross. But he accepted the shame as if it were nothing because of the joy that God put before him. And now he is sitting at the right side of God's throne. Think about Jesus' example. He held on while wicked people were doing evil things to him. So do not get tired and stop trying.

Hebrews 12:1-3 NCV

Therefore we also, since are surrounded by so great a cloud of witnesses, let us lay aside every weight, and the sin which so easily ensnares us, and let us run with endurance the race that is set before us, looking unto Jesus, the author and finisher of our faith, who for the joy that was set before Him endured the cross, despising the shame, and has sat down at the right hand of the throne of God. For consider Him who endured such hostility

from sinners again Himself, lest you become weary and discouraged in your souls.

Hebrews 12:1-3 NKJV

Consider it pure joy, my brothers and sisters, whenever you face trials of many kinds, because you know that the testing of your faith produces perseverance. Let perseverance finish its work so that you may be mature and complete, not lacking anything.

James 1:2-4 NIV

Consider it a sheer gift, friends, when test and challenges come at you from all sides. You know that under pressure, your faith-life is forced into the open and shows its true colors. So don't try to get out of anything prematurely. Let it do its work so you become mature and well-developed, not deficient in any way.

James 1:2-4 MSG

If any of you need to be wise, ask God to make you wise. He gives plenty of wisdom to all people. He is not angry because you ask him. He will make you wise.

But when you ask, you must believe that God will do it. You must not doubt and think, 'Perhaps God will not do it.' A person who doubts is like a wave on the sea. The wind drives it this way and that way.

That person must not think that he will get anything from the Lord.

A person like that has two minds. He cannot go straight in any of his ways.

James 1:5-8 WE

What good is it, my brothers and sisters, if someone claims to have faith but has no deeds? Can such faith save them? Suppose a brother or a sister is without clothes and daily food. If one of you says to them, "Go in peace; keep warm and well fed," but does nothing about their physical needs, what good is it? In the same way, faith by itself, if it is not accompanied by action, is dead.

But someone will say, "You have faith; I have deeds."

Show me your faith without deeds, and I will show you my faith by my deeds. You believe that there is one God. Good!

Even the demons believe that—and shudder.

You foolish person, do you want evidence that faith without deeds is useless?

James 2:14-20 NIV

And the prayer of faith shall save the sick, and the Lord shall raise him up; and if he have committed sins, they shall be forgiven.

James 5:15

And the prayer that is said with faith will make the sick person well; the Lord will heal that person. And if the person has sinned, the sins will be forgiven.

James 5:15 NCV

Blessed be the God and Father of our Lord Jesus Christ, who according to His abundant mercy has begotten us again to a living hope through the resurrection of Jesus Christ from the dead, to an inheritance incorruptible and undefiled and that does not fade away, reserved in heaven for you, who are kept by the power of God through faith for salvation ready to be revealed in the last time.

In this you greatly rejoice, though now for a little while, if need be, you have been grieved by various trials, that the genu-ineness of your faith, being much more precious than gold that perishes,

though it is tested by fire, may be found to praise, honor, and glory at the revelation of Jesus Christ, whom having not seen[a] you love. Though now you do not see Him, yet believing, you rejoice with joy inexpressible and full of glory, receiving the end of your faith—the salvation of your souls.

I Peter 1:3-9 NKJV

I am writing to you who share the same precious faith we have. This faith was given to you because of the justice and fairness of Jesus Christ, our God and Savior.

May God give you more and more grace and peace as you grow in your knowledge of God and Jesus our Lord.

By his divine power, God has given us everything we need for living a godly life. We have received all of this by coming to know him, the one who called us to himself by means of his marvelous glory and excellence. And because of his glory and excellence, he has given us great and precious promises. These are the promises that enable you to share his divine nature and escape the world's corruption caused by human desires.

In view of all this, make every effort to respond to God's

promises. Supplement your faith with a generous provision of moral excellence, and moral excellence with knowledge, and knowledge with self-control, and self-control with patient endurance, and patient endurance with godliness, and godliness with brotherly affection, and brotherly affection with love for everyone.

The more you grow like this, the more productive and useful you will be in your knowledge of our Lord Jesus Christ. But those who fail to develop in this way are shortsighted or blind, forgetting that they have been cleansed from their old sins.

So, dear brothers and sisters, work hard to prove that you really are among those God has called and chosen. Do these things, and you will never fall away.

2 Peter 1:1-10 NLT

For every child of God defeats this evil world, and we achieve this victory through our faith. And who can win this battle against the world? Only those who believe that Jesus is the Son of God.

I John 5:4-5 NLT

My purpose in writing is simply this: that you who believe in God's Son will know beyond the shadow of a doubt that you have eternal life, the reality and not the illusion. And how bold and free we then become in his presence, freely asking according to his will, sure that he's listening. And if we're confident that he's listening, we know that what we've asked for is as good as ours.

I John 5:13-15 MSG

But you, dear friends, by building yourselves up in your most holy faith and praying in the Holy Spirit, keep yourselves in God's love as you wait for the mercy of our Lord Jesus Christ to bring you to eternal life.

Jude 1:20-21 NIV

But dear friends, use your most holy faith to build yourselves up, praying in the Holy Spirit. Keep yourselves in God's love as you wait for the Lord Jesus Christ with his mercy to give you life forever.

Jude 1:20-21 NCV

Protection Scriptures
Old Testament

Some time later, the Lord spoke to Abram in a vision and said to him, "Do not be afraid, Abram, for I will protect you, and your reward will be great."

Genesis 15:1 NLT

I am with you and will watch over you wherever you go, and I will bring you back to this land. I will not leave you until I have done what I have promised you.

Genesis 28:15 NIV

Then the Lord said to Jacob, "Return to the land of your fathers and to your family, and I will be with you."

Genesis 31:3 NKJV

So God sent me here ahead of you to make sure you have some descendants left on earth and to keep you alive in an amazing way.

Genesis 45:7 NCV

Moses spoke to the people: "Don't be afraid. Stand firm and watch God do his work of salvation for you today. Take a good look at the Egyptians today for you're never going to see them again. God will fight the battle for you.

Exodus 14:13,14 MSG

Who is like You, among the gods, O Lord?

Who is like You, majestic in holiness

Awesome in praises, working wonders?

You stretched out Your right hand, The earth swallowed them. "In Your lovingkindness You have led the people whom You have redeemed;

In Your strength You have guided them to Your holy habitation.

Exodus 15:11-13 NASB

Behold, I sent an Angel before thee, to keep thee in the way, and to bring thee into the place which I have prepared.

Exodus 23:20

I will send My fear before you, I will cause confusion among all the people to whom you come, and will make all your enemies turn their backs to you.

Exodus 23:27 NKJV

And if the Lord is pleased with us, he will bring us safely into that land and give it to us. It is a rich land flowing with milk and honey. Do not rebel against the Lord, and don't be afraid of the people of the land. They are only helpless prey to us! They have no protection, but the Lord is with us! Don't be afraid of them!

Numbers 14:8-9 NLT

Then I said to you, "Do not be terrified; do not be afraid of them. The Lord your God, who is going before you, will fight for you, as he did for you in Egypt, before your very eyes, and in the wilderness. There you saw how the Lord your God carried you, as a father carries his son, all the way you went until you reached this place."

Deuteronomy 1:29-31 NIV

Do not be afraid of the nations there, for the Lord your God will fight for you.

Deuteronomy 3:22 NLT

The Lord ordered us to obey all these commands and to respect the Lord our God so that we will always do well and stay alive, as we are today.

Deuteronomy 6:24 NCV

When you go to war against your enemies and see horses and chariots and an army greater than yours, do not be afraid of them, because the LORD your God, who brought you up out of Egypt, will be with you. When you are about to go into battle, the priest shall come forward and address the army. He shall say: "Hear, Israel: Today you are going into battle against your enemies. Do not be fainthearted or afraid; do not panic or be terrified by them. For the LORD your God is the one who goes with you to fight for you against your enemies to give you victory."

Deuteronomy 20:1-4 NIV

If you fully obey the LORD your God and carefully follow all his commands I give you today, the LORD your God will set you high above all the nations on earth. All these blessings will come on you and accompany you if you obey the LORD your God:

The LORD will grant that the enemies who rise up against you will be defeated before you. They will come at you from one direction but flee from you in seven.

The LORD will establish you as his holy people, as he promised you on oath, if you keep the commands of the LORD your God and walk in obedience to him.

Deuteronomy 28:1,2,7,9 NIV

Be strong and of a good courage, fear not, nor be afraid of them: for the Lord thy God, he it is that doth go with thee; he will not fail thee, nor forsake thee.

Deuteronomy 31:6

Moses said this about the tribe of Benjamin: "The people of Benjamin are loved by the Lord and live in safety beside him. He surrounds them continuously and preserves them from every harm."

Deuteronomy 33:12 NLT

The everlasting God is your place of safety, and his arms will hold you up forever. He will force your enemy out ahead of you, saying, 'Destroy the enemy!'

Deuteronomy 33:27 NCV

Be strong and courageous, because you will lead these people to inherit the land I swore to their ancestors to give them.

Be strong and very courageous. Be careful to obey all the law my servant Moses gave you; do not turn from it to the right or to the left, that you may be successful wherever you go. Keep this Book of the Law always on your lips; mediate on it day and night, so that you may be careful to do everything written in it. Then you will be prosperous and successful.

Joshua 1:6-8 NIV

For it is the Lord our God Who brought us and our fathers up out of the land of Egypt, from the house of bondage, Who did those great signs in our sight and preserved us in all the way that we went and among all the peoples through whom we passed.

And the Lord drove out before us all the people, the Amorites who dwelt in the land. Therefore we also will serve the Lord, for He is our God.

Joshua 24:17-18 AMP

Stay with me; do not fear. For he who seeks my life seeks your life, but with me you shall be safe."

I Samuel 22:23 NKJV

He said:

"The LORD is my rock, my fortress and my deliverer;

my God is my rock, in whom I take refuge,

my shield and the horn of my salvation.

He is my stronghold, my refuge and my savior—

from violent people you save me.

"I called to the LORD, who is worthy of praise,

and have been saved from my enemies.

2 Samuel 22:2-4 NIV

But in my distress I cried out to the Lord; yes, I cried to my God for help. He heard me from his sanctuary; my cry reached his ears.

2 Samuel 22:7 NLT

"For You are my lamp, O LORD;

The LORD shall enlighten my darkness.

For by You I can run against a troop;

By my God I can leap over a wall.

As for God, His way is perfect;

The word of the LORD is proven;

He is a shield to all who trust in Him.

"For who is God, except the LORD?

And who is a rock, except our God?

God is my strength and power,

And He makes my way perfect.

He makes my feet like the feet of deer,

And sets me on my high places.

He teaches my hands to make war,

So that my arms can bend a bow of bronze.

"You have also given me the shield of Your salvation;

Your gentleness has made me great.

You enlarged my path under me;

So my feet did not slip.

2 Samuel 22:29-37 NKJV

You armed me with strength for battle; you humbled my adversaries before me. You made my enemies turn their backs in flight, and I destroyed by foes.

2 Samuel 22:40-41 NIV

God give me victory over my enemies and brings people under my rule. He frees me from my enemies.

"You set me over those who hate me. You saved me from violent people.

Samuel 22:48-49 NCV

"Don't be afraid," the prophet answered. "Those who are with us are more than those who are with them."

Kings 6:16 NIV

Jabez prayed to the God of Israel, "Please do good things for me and give me more land. Stay with me, and don't let anyone hurt me. Then I won't have any pain." And God did what Jabez had asked.

I Chronicles 4:10 NCV

"Be strong and brave. Don't be afraid or worried because of the king of Assyria or his large army. There is a greater power with us than with him. He only has men, but we have the lord our God to help us and to fight our battles." The people were encouraged by the words of Hezekiah king of Judah.

Chronicles 32:7-8 NCV

On the twelfth day of the first month we set out from the Ahava Canal to go to Jerusalem. The hand of our God was on us, and he protected us from enemies and bandits along the way.

Ezra 8:31 NIV

So on October 2 the wall was finished – just fifty-two days after we had begun. When our enemies and the surrounding nations heard about it, they were frightened and humiliated. They realized this work had been done with the help of our God.

Nehemiah 6:15-16 NLT

You will feel safe because there is hope; you will look around and rest in safety.

You will lie down, and no one will scare you. Many people will want favors from you.

Job 11:18-19 NCV

But you, Lord, are a shield around me, my glory, the One who lifts my head high. I call out to the Lord, and he answers me from his holy mountain.

I lie down and sleep; I wake again, because the Lord sustains me. I will not fear though tens of thousands assail me on every side.

Arise, Lord! Deliver me, my God! Strike all my enemies on the jaw; break the teeth of the wicked.

Psalm 3:3-7 NIV

In peace I will lie down and sleep, for you alone, O Lord, will keep me safe.

Psalm 4:8 NLT

Lead me, O Lord, in Your righteousness because of my enemies; Make Your way straight before my face.

Psalm 5:8 NKJV

But let all those that put their trust in thee rejoice: let them ever shout for joy, because thou defendest them: let them also that love thy name be joyful in thee.

For thou, Lord, wilt bless the righteous; with favour wilt thou compass him as with a shield.

Psalm 5:11,12

Lord my God, I take refuge in you; save and deliver me from all who pursue me

Psalm 7:1 NIV

God protects me like a shield; he saves those whose hearts are right.

Psalm 7:10 NCV

The Lord also will be a refuge for the oppressed, a refuge in times of trouble.

Psalm 9:9

The Lord replies, "I have seen violence done to the helpless, and I have heard the groans of the poor. Now I will rise up to rescue them, as they have longed for me to do." The Lord's promises are pure, like silver refined in a furnace, purified seven times over.

Psalm 12:5-6 NLT

Preserve me, O God, for in You I put my trust.

Psalm 16:1 NKJV

I love you, God – you make me strong. God is bedrock under my feet, the castle in which I live, my rescuing knight. My God – the high crag where I run for dear life, hiding behind the boulders, safe in the granite hideout.

I sing to God, the Praise-Lofty, and find myself safe and saved.

Psalm 18:2-3 MSG

He rescued me from my powerful enemy, from my foes, who were too strong for me. They confronted me in the day of my disaster, but the Lord was my support. He brought me out into a spacious place; he rescued me because he delighted in me.

Psalm 18:17-19 NIV

For You cause my lamp to be lighted and to shine; the Lord my God illumines my darkness.

For by You I can run through a troop, and by my God I can leap over a wall.

As for God, His way is perfect! The word of the Lord is tested and tried; He is a shield to all those who take refuge and put their trust in Him.

For who is God except the Lord? Or who is the Rock save our God,

The God who girds me with strength and makes my way perfect?

He makes my feet like hinds' feet [able to stand firmly or make progress on the dangerous heights of testing and trouble]; He sets me securely upon my high places.

He teaches my hands to war, so that my arms can bend a bow of bronze.

You have also given me the shield of Your salvation, and Your right hand has held me up; Your gentleness and conde-scension have made me great.

You have given plenty of room for my steps under me, that my feet would not slip.

Psalm 18:28-36 AMP

He is the God who pays back those who harm me; he subdues the nations under me and rescues me from my enemies.

You hold me safe beyond the reach of my enemies; you save me from violent opponents.

Psalm 18:47-48 NLT

Now I know that the Lord saves His anointed; He will answer him from His holy heaven with the saving strength of His right hand.

Some trust in chariots, and some in horses; But we will remember the name of the Lord our God.

Psalm 20:6-7 NKJV

The king truly trusts the Lord. Because God Most High always loves him, he will not be overwhelmed.

Psalm 21:7 NCV

For he has not ignored or belittled the suffering of the needy. He has not turned his back on them, but has listened to their cries for help.

Psalm 22:24 NLT

The LORD is my shepherd, I lack nothing.

He makes me lie down in green pastures,

he leads me beside quiet waters,

he refreshes my soul.

He guides me along the right paths

for his name's sake.

Even though I walk

through the darkest valley,

I will fear no evil,

for you are with me;

your rod and your staff,

they comfort me.

You prepare a table before me

in the presence of my enemies.

You anoint my head with oil;

my cup overflows.

Surely your goodness and love will follow me

all the days of my life,

and I will dwell in the house of the LORD

forever

Psalm 23:1-6 NIV

O my God, I trust in You; Let me not be ashamed; Let not my enemies triumph over me.

Show me Your ways, O Lord; teach me Your paths. Lead me in Your truth and teach me, For You are the God of my salvation; on You I wait all the day.

Psalm 25:4-5 NKJV

The Lord leads with unfailing love and faithfulness all who keep his covenant and obey his demands.

Psalm 25:10 NLT

May integrity and uprightness protect me, because my hope, Lord, is in you.

Deliver Israel, O God, from all their troubles!

Psalm 25:21-22 NIV

Lord, I trust you. I have said, "You are my God." Lord, I called to you, so do not let me be disgraced. Let the wicked be disgraced and lie silent in the grave.

Psalm 31:17 NCV

How great is your goodness that you have stored up for those who fear you, that you have given to those who trust you.

You do this for all to see.

You protect them by your presence from what people plan against them. You shelter them from evil words.

Psalm 31:19-20 NCV

Love God, all you saints; God takes care of all who stay close to him, But he pays back in full those arrogant enough to go it alone.

Psalm 31:23 MSG

For you are my hiding place; you protect me from trouble. You surround me with songs of victory.

The Lord says, "I will guide you along the best pathway for your life. I will advise you and watch over you.

Psalm 32:7-8 NLT

We wait in hope for the Lord' he is our help and our shield. In him our hearts rejoice, for we trust in his holy name.

Psalm 33:20-21 NIV

This poor man called, and the Lord heard him and saved him from all his troubles.

The angel of the Lord camps around those who fear God, and he saves them.

Psalm 34:6-7 NCV

The eyes of the LORD are upon the righteous, and his ears are open unto their cry.

The face of the LORD is against them that do evil, to cut off the remembrance of them from the earth.

The righteous cry, and the LORD heareth, and delivereth them out of all their troubles.

The LORD is nigh unto them that are of a broken heart; and saveth such as be of a contrite spirit.

Many are the afflictions of the righteous: but the LORD delivereth him out of them all.

He keepeth all his bones: not one of them is broken.

Evil shall slay the wicked: and they that hate the righteous shall be desolate.

The LORD redeemeth the soul of his servants: and none of them that trust in him shall be desolate

Psalm 34:15-22 KJV

LORD, battle with those who battle with me.

Fight against those who fight against me.

Pick up the shield and armor.

Rise up and help me.

Lift up your spears, both large and small,

against those who chase me.

Tell me, "I will save you."

Make those who want to kill me

be ashamed and disgraced.

Make those who plan to harm me

turn back and run away.

Psalm 35:1-4 NCV

Trust in the LORD and do good.

Then you will live safely in the land and prosper.

Take delight in the LORD,

and he will give you your heart's desires.

Commit everything you do to the LORD.

Trust him, and he will help you.

He will make your innocence radiate like the dawn,

and the justice of your cause will shine like the noonday

sun.

Be still in the presence of the LORD,

and wait patiently for him to act.

Don't worry about evil people who prosper

or fret about their wicked schemes.

Stop being angry!

Turn from your rage!

Do not lose your temper—

it only leads to harm.

For the wicked will be destroyed,

but those who trust in the LORD will possess the land.

Soon the wicked will disappear.

Though you look for them, they will be gone.

The lowly will possess the land

and will live in peace and prosperity.

Psalm 37:3-11 NLT

The Lord makes firm the steps of the one who delights in him; though he may stumble, he will not fall, for the Lord upholds him with his hand.

Psalm 37:23-24 NIV

For the Lord loves justice, and does not forsake His saints; they are preserved forever, but the descendants of the wicked shall be cut off.

Psalm 37:28 NKJV

The Lord saves good people; he is their strength in times of trouble. The Lord helps them and saves them; he saves them from the wicked, because they trust in him for protection.

Psalm 37:39-40 NCV

I waited patiently for the Lord; he turned to me and heard my cry. He lifted me out of the slimy pit, out of the mud and mire; he set my feet on a rock and gave me a firm place to stand.

Psalm 40:1-2 NIV

And me? I'm a mess. I'm nothing and have nothing: make something of me. You can do it; you've got what it takes – but God, don't put it off.

Psalm 40:17 MSG

Happy are those who think about the poor. When trouble comes, the Lord will save them. The Lord will protect them and spare their life and will bless them in the land. He will not let their enemies take them.

Psalm 41:1-2 NCV

I know that you are pleased with me, for my enemy does not triumph over me. Because of my integrity you uphold me and set me in your presence forever.

Psalm 41:11-12 NIV

Through You we will push down our enemies; Through Your name we will trample those who rise up against us. For I will not trust in my bow, nor shall my sword save me. But You have saved us from our enemies, and have put to shame those who hated us.

Psalm 44:5-7 NKJV

God is our refuge and strength, an ever present help in trouble.

Therefore we will not fear, though the earth give way and the mountains fall into the heart of the sea, though its waters roar and foam and the mountains quake with their surging.

Psalm 46:1-3 NIV

The LORD Almighty is with us;

   the God of Jacob is our fortress.

Come and see what the LORD has done,

   the desolations he has brought on the earth.

He makes wars cease

   to the ends of the earth.

He breaks the bow and shatters the spear;

   he burns the shields[a] with fire.

He says, "Be still, and know that I am God;

   I will be exalted among the nations,

   I will be exalted in the earth."

Psalm 46:7-10 NIV

Then call on me when you are in trouble, and I will rescue
you, and you will give me glory.

Psalm 50:15 NLT

See, God will help me; the Lord will support me.

Let my enemies be punished with their own evil.

Destroy them because you are loyal to me.

Psalm 54:4-5 NCV

As for me, I will call upon God, and the Lord shall save me. Evening and morning and at noon I will pray, and cry aloud. And He shall hear my voice.

He has redeemed my soul in peace from the battle that was against me, for there were many against me.

Psalm 55:16-18 NKJV

Cast your cares on the Lord and he will sustain you; he will never let the righteous be shaken.

Psalm 55:22 NIV

What time I am afraid, I will trust in thee.

In God I will praise his word, in God I have put my trust; I will not fear what flesh can do unto me...

In God have I put my trust; I will not be afraid what man can do unto me

Psalm 56:3,4,11

My heart is fixed, O God, my heart is steadfast and confident! I will sing and make melody.

Psalm 57:7 AMP

Deliver me from my enemies, O God; be my fortress against those who are attacking me.

Psalm 59:1 NIV

You are my strength; I wait for you to rescue me, for you, O God, are my fortress.

In his unfailing love, my God will stand with me. He will let me look down in triumph on all my enemies.

Psalm 59:9-10 NLT

But I will sing of your strength, in the morning I will sing of your love; for you are my fortress, my refuge in times of trouble.

You are my strength, I sing praise to you; you, God, are my fortress, my God on whom I can rely.

Psalm 59:16-17 NIV

I wait quietly before God, for my victory comes from him. He alone is my rock and my salvation, my fortress where I will never be shaken.

Psalm 62:1-2 NLT

Yes, my soul, find rest in God;

  my hope comes from him.

Truly he is my rock and my salvation;

  he is my fortress, I will not be shaken.

My salvation and my honor depend on God[a];

  he is my mighty rock, my refuge.

Trust in him at all times, you people;

  pour out your hearts to him,

    for God is our refuge.

Psalm 62:5-8 NIV

But as for me, my prayer is to You,

O LORD, in the acceptable time;

O God, in the multitude of Your mercy,

Hear me in the truth of Your salvation.

 Deliver me out of the mire,

And let me not sink;

Let me be delivered from those who hate me,

And out of the deep waters.

15 Let not the floodwater overflow me,

Nor let the deep swallow me up;

And let not the pit shut its mouth on me.

Hear me, O LORD, for Your lovingkindness is good;

Turn to me according to the multitude of Your tender mercies.

And do not hide Your face from Your servant,

For I am in trouble;

Hear me speedily.

Draw near to my soul, and redeem it;

Deliver me because of my enemies.

Psalm 69:13-18 NKJV

He will rescue the poor when they cry to him; he will help the oppressed, who have no one to defend them. He feels pity for the

weak and the needy, and he will rescue them.

Psalm 72:12-13 NLT

God, look at our shield; be kind to your appointed king.

One day in the courtyards of your Temple is better than a thousand days anywhere else. I would rather be a doorkeeper in the Temple of my God than live in the homes of the wicked. The Lord God is like a sun and shield; the Lord give us kindness and honor. He does not hold back anything good from those whose lives are innocent. Lord All-Powerful, happy are the people who trust you!

Psalm 84:9-2 NCV

For great is your love toward me; you have delivered me from the depths, from the realm of the dead.

Psalm 86:13 NIV

Those who live in the shelter of the Most High will find rest in the shadow of the Almighty.

This I declare about the LORD: He alone is my refuge, my place of safety; he is my God, and I trust him.

For he will rescue you from every trap and protect you from deadly disease.

He will cover you with his feathers. He will shelter you with his wings. His faithful promises are your armor and protection.

Do not be afraid of the terrors of the night, nor the arrow that flies in the day.

Do not dread the disease that stalks in darkness, nor the disaster that strikes at midday.

Though a thousand fall at your side, though ten thousand are dying around you, these evils will not touch you.

Just open your eyes, and see how the wicked are punished.

If you make the LORD your refuge, if you make the Most High your shelter,

no evil will conquer you; no plague will come near your home.

For he will order his angels to protect you wherever you go.

They will hold you up with their hands so you won't even hurt your foot on a stone.

You will trample upon lions and cobras; you will crush fierce lions and serpents under your feet!

The LORD says, "I will rescue those who love me. I will protect those who trust in my name.

When they call on me, I will answer; I will be with them in trouble. I will rescue and honor them.

I will reward them with a long life and give them my salvation."

Psalm 91:1-16 NLT

Unless the Lord had been my help, My soul would soon have settled in silence.

If I say, "My foot slips," Your mercy, O Lord, will hold me up.

Psalm 94:17-18 NKJV

But the Lord is my defender; my God is the rock of my protection.

Psalm 94:22 NCV

O sing to the Lord a new song; sing to the Lord, all the earth!
Sing to the Lord, bless (affectionately praise) His name; show forth His salvation from day to day.

Psalm 96:1-2 AMP

Let those who love the Lord hate evil, for he guards the lives of his faithful ones and delivers them from the hand of the wicked.

Psalm 97:10 NIV

Save us, God, our God! Gather us back out of exile so we can give thanks to your holy name and join in the glory when you are praised!

Psalm 106:47 MSG

"Lord, help!" they cried in their trouble, and he rescued them from their distress. He led them straight to safety.

Psalm 107:6,7 NLT

Then they cried to the Lord in their trouble, and he saved them from their distress. He brought them out of darkness, the utter darkness, and broke away their chains.

Psalm 107:13-14 NIV

Then they cried out to the Lord in their trouble, and He saved them out of their distresses.

He sent His word and healed them, and delivered them from their destructions.

Psalm 107:19-20 NKJV

Be exalted, O God, above the heavens; let your glory be over all the earth.

Save us and help us with your right hand, that those you love may be delivered.

Psalm 108:5-6 NIV

Give us help for the hard task; human help is worthless. In God we'll do our very best; he'll flatten the opposition for good.

Psalm 108:12-13 MSG

Such people will not be overcome by evil. Those who are righteous will be long remembered. They do not fear bad news; they confidently trust the Lord to care for them. They are confident and fearless and can face their foes triumphantly.

Psalm 112:6-8 NLT

O Israel, trust in the LORD; He is their help and their shield.

O house of Aaron, trust in the LORD; He is their help and their shield.

You who fear the LORD, trust in the LORD; He is their help and their shield.

The LORD has been mindful of us; He will bless us; He will bless the house of Israel; He will bless the house of Aaron.

He will bless those who fear the LORD, Both small and great.

Psalm 115:9-13 NKJV

When hard pressed, I cried to the LORD; he brought me into a spacious place.

The LORD is with me; I will not be afraid. What can mere mortals do to me?

The LORD is with me; he is my helper. I look in triumph on my enemies.

It is better to take refuge in the LORD than to trust in humans.

It is better to take refuge in the LORD than to trust in princes.

All the nations surrounded me, but in the name of the LORD I cut them down.

They surrounded me on every side, but in the name of the LORD I cut them down.

They swarmed around me like bees, but they were consumed as quickly as burning thorns; in the name of the LORD I cut them down.

I was pushed back and about to fall, but the LORD helped me.

The LORD is my strength and my defense; he has become my salvation.

Shouts of joy and victory resound in the tents of the righteous: "The LORD's right hand has done mighty things!

The LORD's right hand is lifted high; the LORD's right hand has done mighty things!"

Psalm 118:5-16 NIV

You are my refuge and my shield; your word is my source of hope.

Get out of my life, you evil-minded people, for I intend to

obey the commands of my God.

LORD, sustain me as you promised, that I may live! Do not let my hope be crushed.

Sustain me, and I will be rescued; then I will meditate continually on your decrees

Psalm 119:114-117 NLT

I lift up my eyes to the mountains –where does my help come from?

My help comes from the Lord, the Maker of heaven and earth.

He will not let your foot slip – he who watches over you will not slumber; indeed, he who watches over Israel will neither slumber no sleep.

The Lord watches over you – the Lord is your shade at your right hand; the sun will not harm you by day, nor the moon by night.

The Lord will keep you from all harm – he will watch over your life; the Lord will watch over your coming and going both now and forevermore.

Psalm 121:1-8 NIV

Those who trust in the Lord are like Mount Zion, which cannot be moved, but abides forever. As the mountains surround Jerusalem, so the Lord surrounds His people from this time forth and forever.

Psalm 125:1-2 NKJV

Happy are those who respect the Lord and obey him. You will enjoy what you work for, and you will be blessed with good things.

Psalm 128:1-2 NCV

But the Lord is righteous; he has cut me free from the cords of the wicked.

Psalm 129:4 NIV

His enemies will I clothe with shame, but upon himself shall his crown flourish.

Psalm 132:18 AMP

Though I walk in the midst of trouble, thou wilt revive me: thou shalt stretch forth thine hand against the wrath of mine enemies, and thy right hand shall save me.

Psalm 138:7

Rescue me, Lord from evildoers; protect me from the violent.

Keep me safe, Lord, from the hands of the wicked; protect me from the violent, who devise ways to trip my feet.

Sovereign Lord, my strong deliverer, you shield my head in the day of battle.

Psalm 140:1,4,7 NIV

Surely righteous people are praising your name; the godly will live in your presence.

Psalm 140:13 NLT

Rescue me from my enemies, LORD, for I hide myself in you.

Teach me to do your will, for you are my God; may your good Spirit lead me on level ground.

For your name's sake, LORD, preserve my life; in your righteousness, bring me out of trouble.

In your unfailing love, silence my enemies; destroy all my foes, for I am your servant.

Psalm 143:9-12 NIV

Blessed be the Lord, my Rock and my keen and firm Strength, Who teaches my hands to war and my fingers to fight.

My Steadfast Love and my Fortress, my High Tower and my Delivered, my Shield and He in Whom I trust and take refuge, Who subdues my people under me.

Psalm 144:1-2 AMP

The Lord helps those who have been defeated and takes care of those who are in trouble.

Psalm 145:14 NCV

The Lord is close to all who call on him, yes, to all who call on him in truth.

He grants the desires of those who fear him; he hears their cries for help and rescues them.

The Lord protects all those who love him, but he destroys the wicked.

Psalm 145:18-20 NLT

But whoever listens to me will live in safety and be at ease, without fear of harm.

Proverbs 1:33 NIV

He stores up sound wisdom for the upright; He is a shield to those who walk in integrity,

Guarding the paths of justice, and He preserves the way of His godly ones.

Proverbs 2:7-8 NASB

Discretion will preserve you; Understanding will keep you, to deliver you from the way of evil, from the man who speaks perverse things, from those who leave the paths of uprightness to walk in the ways of darkness.

Proverbs 2:11-13 NKJV

My son, do not let wisdom and understanding out of your sight, preserve sound judgment and discretion; they will be life for you, an ornament to grace your neck.

Then you will go on your way in safety, and your foot will not stumble. When you lie down, you will not be afraid; when you lie down, your sleep will be sweet.

Have no fear of sudden disaster or of the ruin that overtakes the wicked, for the Lord will be at your side and will keep your foot from being snared.

Proverbs 3:21-26 NIV

Don't turn your back on wisdom, for she will protect you.
Love her, and she will guard you.

Proverbs 4:6 NLT

The righteous will never be uprooted, but the wicked will not
remain in the land.

Proverbs 10:30 NIV

The integrity of the upright shall guide them.

Proverbs 11:3

The good person is saved from trouble; it comes to the
wicked instead.

Proverbs 11:8 NCV

The one who guards his mouth preserves his life; the one who
opens wide his lips comes to ruin.

Proverbs 13:3 NASB

The lips of the wise shall preserve them.

Proverbs 14:3

Those who fear the Lord are secure; he will be a refuge for their children.

Fear of the Lord is a life-giving fountain; it offers escape from the snares of death.

Proverbs 14:26-27 NLT

Those who disregard discipline despise themselves, but the one who heeds correction gains understanding.

Proverbs 15:32 NIV

Pride leads to destruction; a proud attitude brings ruin.

It is better to be humble and be with those who suffer than to share stolen property with the proud.

Proverbs 16:18-19 NCV

The lips of fools bring them strife, and their mouths invite a beating.

Proverbs 18:6 NIV

The name of the Lord is a strong tower; the righteous run to it and are safe

Proverbs 18:10 NKJV

Don't say, "I will get even for this wrong." Wait for the Lord to handle the matter.

Proverbs 20:22 NLT

A man's steps are of the Lord; how then can a man understand his own way?

Proverbs 20:24 NKJV

You can get the horses ready for battle, but it is the Lord who gives the victory.

Proverbs 21:31 NCV

The fear of man brings a snare, but whoever trusts in the Lord shall be safe.

Proverbs 29:25 NKJV

Every word of God is flawless; he is a shield to those who take refuge in him.

Proverbs 30:5 NIV

For thou hast been a strength to the poor, a strength to the needy in his distress, a refuge from the storm, a shadow from the heat, when the blast of the terrible ones is as a storm against the wall.

Isaiah 25:4

Your ears will hear a word behind you, "This is the way, walk in it," whenever you turn to the right or to the left.

Isaiah 30:21 NASB

My people will live in safety, quietly at home.
They will be at rest.

Isaiah 32:18 NLT

Lord, be gracious to us; we long for you. Be our strength every morning, our salvation in time of distress.

Isaiah 33:2 NIV

Strengthen the weak hands, and make firm the feeble knees. Say to those who are fearful-hearted, "Be strong, do not fear! Behold, your God will come with vengeance, with the recompense of God; He will come and save you."

Isaiah 35:3-4 NKJV

Don't panic. I'm with you. There's no need to fear for I'm your God. I'll give you strength. I'll help you. I'll hold you steady, keep a firm grip on you.

Count on it: Everyone who had it in for you will end up out in the cold – real losers. Those who worked against you will end up empty handed – nothing to show for their lives.

When you go out looking for your old adversaries you won't find them- not a trace of your old enemies, note even a memory.

That's right. Because I, your God, have a firm grip on you and I'm not letting go. I'm telling you, 'Don't panic. I'm right here to help you.'

Isaiah 41:10-13 MSG

Then I will lead the blind along a way they never knew; I will guide them along paths they have not known. I will make the darkness become light for them, and the rough ground smooth. These are the things I will do; I will not leave my people.

Isaiah 42:16 NCV

Do not fear, for I have redeemed you; I have summoned you by name; you are mine. When you pass through the waters, I will be with you; and when you pass through the rivers, they will not sweep over you. When you walk through the fire, you will not be burned; the flames will not set you ablaze.

Isaiah 43:1-2 NIV

Do not tremble; do not be afraid. Did I not proclaim my purposes for you long ago? You are my witnesses – is there any other God? No! There is no other Rock – not one!

Isaiah 44:8 NLT

This is what the Lord says:

"In the time of my favor I will answer you, and in the day of salvation I will help you; I will keep you and will make you to be a covenant for the people, to restore the land and to reassign its desolate inheritances, to say to the captives, 'Come out,' and to those in darkness, 'Be free!'

"They will feed beside the roads and find pasture on every barren hill. They will neither hunger nor thirst, nor will the desert heat or the sun beat down on them. He who has compassion on them will guide them and lead them beside springs of water.

Isaiah 49:8-10 NIV

I, even I, am He who comforts you. Who are you that you should be afraid of a man who will die, and of the son of a man who will be made like grass?

Isaiah 51:12 NKJV

I have put my words in your mouth and covered you with the shadow of my hand – I who set the heavens in place, who laid the foundations of the earth, and who say to Zion, 'You are my people."

Isaiah 51:16 NIV

The Lord has demonstrated his holy power before the eyes of all the nations. All the ends of the earth will see the victory of our God.

Isaiah 52:10 NLT

Though the mountains be shaken and the hills be removed, yet my unfailing love for you will not be shaken nor my covenant of peace be removed, says the Lord, who has compassion on you.

Isaiah 54:10 NIV

I will build you using fairness. You will be safe from those who would hurt you, so you will have nothing to fear. Nothing willcome to make you afraid. I will not send anyone to attack you, and you will defeat those who do attack you.

Isaiah 54:14-15 NCV

So no weapon that is used against you will defeat you. You will show that those who speak against you are wrong. These are the good things my servants receive. Their victory comes from me, says the Lord.

Isaiah 54:17 NCV

The Lord will guide you always; he will satisfy your needs in a sun-scorched land and will strengthen your frame. You will be like a well-watered garden, like a spring whose waters never fail.

Isaiah 58:11 NIV

Listen! The Lord's arm is not too weak to save you, nor is his ear too deaf to hear you call.

Isaiah 59:1 NLT

For He put on righteousness as a breastplate, And a helmet of salvation on His head; He put on the garments of vengeance for clothing, And was clad with zeal as a cloak.

According to their deeds, accordingly He will repay, Fury to His adversaries, Recompense to His enemies; The coastlands He will fully repay.

So shall they fear The name of the LORD from the west, And His glory from the rising of the sun; When the enemy comes in like a flood, The Spirit of the LORD will lift up a standard against him.

"The Redeemer will come to Zion, And to those who turn from transgression in Jacob," Says the LORD.

"As for Me," says the LORD, "this is My covenant with them: My Spirit who is upon you, and My words which I have put in your mouth, shall not depart from your mouth, nor from the mouth of your descendants, nor from the mouth of your descendants' descendants," says the LORD, "from this time and forevermore."

Isaiah 59:17-21 NKJV

They will fight against you like an attacking army, but I will make you as secure as a fortified wall of bronze. They will not conquer you, for I am with you to protect and rescue you. I, the Lord, have spoken!

Yes, I will certainly keep you from these wicked men. I will rescue you from their cruel hands.

Jeremiah 15:20-21 NLT

But blessed is the one who trusts in the Lord, whose confidence is in him. They will be like a tree planted by the water that sends out its roots by the stream. It does not fear when heat comes; its leaves are always green. It has no worries in a year of drought and never fails to bear fruit.

Jeremiah 17:7-8 NIV

But the Lord is with me as a mighty, awesome One. Therefore my persecutors will stumble, and will not prevail. They will be greatly ashamed, for they will not prosper. Their everlasting confusion will never be forgotten.

Jeremiah 20:11 NKJV

"I sent my people to other countries, but I will gather those who are left alive and bring them back to their own country. Then they will have many children and grow in number. I will place new leaders over my people who will take care of them. And my people will not be afraid or terrified again, and none of them will be lost," says the Lord.

Jeremiah 23:3-4 NCV

But I will deliver you on that day," declares the LORD, "and you will not be given into the hand of the men whom you dread. 18 For I will certainly rescue you, and you will not fall by the sword; but you will have your own life as booty, because you have trusted in Me," declares the LORD.'

Jeremiah 39:17-18 NASB

They will live safely in Israel and build homes and plant vineyards. And when I punish the neighboring nations that treated them with contempt, they will know that I am the Lord their God.

Ezekiel 28:26 NLT

Then King Nebuchadnezzar leaped to his feet in amazement and asked his advisers, "Weren't there three men that we tied up and threw into the fire?"

They replied, "Certainly, Your Majesty."

He said, "Look! I see four men walking around in the fire, unbound and unharmed, and the fourth looks like a son of the gods."

Then Nebuchadnezzar said, "Praise be to the God of Shadrach, Meshach and Abednego, who has sent his angel and rescued his servants! They trusted in him and defied the king's command and were willing to give up their lives rather than serve or worship any god except their own God. Therefore I decree that the people of any nation or language who say anything against the God of Shadrach, Meshach and Abednego be cut into pieces and their houses be turned into piles of rubble, for no other god can save in this way.

Daniel 3:24-25; 28-29 NIV

"Don't be afraid," he said, "for you are very precious to God. Peace! Be encouraged! Be strong!"

As he spoke these words to me, I suddenly felt stronger and said to him, "Please speak to me, my lord, for you have strengthened me."

Daniel 10:19 NLT

But I will show love to the people of Judah. I will free them from their enemies – not with weapons and armies or horses and charioteers, but by my power as the Lord their God.

Hosea 1:7 NLT

At that time, I will make an agreement for them with the wild animals, the birds, and the crawling things. I will smash from the land the bow and the sword and the weapons of war, so my people will live in safety.

Hosea 2:8 NCV

And it shall come to pass that whoever calls on the name of the Lord shall be saved. For in Mount Zion and in Jerusalem there shall be deliverance. As the Lord has said, among the remnant whom the Lord calls.

Joel 2:32 NKJV

As for me, I look to the Lord for help. I wait confidently for God to save me, and my God will certainly hear me. Do not gloat over me, my enemies! For though I fall, I will rise again. Though I sit in darkness, the Lord will be my light.

Micah 7:7-8 NLT

The Lord is good, a refuge in times of trouble. He cares for those who trust in him.

Nahum 1:7 NIV

The Lord will completely destroy anyone making plans against him. Trouble will not come a second time.

Nahum 1:9 NCV

Your GOD is present among you, a strong Warrior there to save you. Happy to have you back, he'll calm you with his love and delight you with his songs.

"The accumulated sorrows of your exile will dissipate. I, your God, will get rid of them for you. You've carried those burdens long enough. At the same time, I'll get rid of all those who've made your life miserable. I'll heal the maimed; I'll bring home the homeless. In the very countries where they were hated they will be venerated. On Judgment Day I'll bring you back home—a great family gathering! You'll be famous and honored all over the world. You'll see it with your own eyes—all those painful partings turned into reunions!" GOD's Promise.

Zephaniah 3:17-20 MSG

And I will rebuke the devourer for your sakes, and he shall not destroy the fruits of your ground neither shall your vine cast her fruit before the time in the field, saith the Lord of hosts.

Malachi 3:11

PROTECTION SCRIPTURES
NEW TESTAMENT

This is how the birth of Jesus the Messiah came about: His mother Mary was pledged to be married to Joseph, but before they came together, she was found to be pregnant through the Holy Spirit. Because Joseph her husband was faithful to the law, and yet did not want to expose her to public disgrace, he had in mind to divorce her quietly.

But after he had considered this, an angel of the Lord appeared to him in a dream and said, "Joseph son of David, do not be afraid to take Mary home as your wife, because what is conceived in her is from the Holy Spirit. She will give birth to a son, and you are to give him the name Jesus, because he will save his people from their sins."

All this took place to fulfill what the Lord had said through the prophet: "The virgin will conceive and give birth to a son, and they will call him Immanuel" (which means "God with us").

When Joseph woke up, he did what the angel of the Lord had commanded him and took Mary home as his wife. But he did not consummate their marriage until she gave birth to a son. And he gave him the name Jesus.

Matthew 1:18-25 NIV

Then Herod called for a private meeting with the wise men, and he learned from them the time when the star first appeared. Then he told them, "Go to Bethlehem and search carefully for the child. And when you find him, come back and tell me so that I can go and worship him, too!"

After this interview the wise men went their way. And the star they had seen in the east guided them to Bethlehem. It went ahead of them and stopped over the place where the child was. When they saw the star, they were filled with joy! They entered the house and saw the child with his mother, Mary, and they bowed down and worshiped him. Then they opened their treasure chests and gave him gifts of gold, frankincense, and myrrh.

When it was time to leave, they returned to their own country by another route, for God had warned them in a dream not to return to Herod.

After the wise men were gone, an angel of the Lord appeared to Joseph in a dream. "Get up! Flee to Egypt with the child and his mother," the angel said. "Stay there until I tell you to return, because Herod is going to search for the child to kill him."

That night Joseph left for Egypt with the child and Mary, his mother, and they stayed there until Herod's death. This fulfilled what the Lord had spoken through the prophet: "I called my Son out of Egypt.

Matthew 2:7-15 NLT

After Herod died, an angel of the Lord appeared in a dream to Joseph in Egypt and said, "Get up, take the child and his mother and go to the land of Israel, for those who were trying to take the child's life are dead."

So he got up, took the child and his mother and went to the land of Israel. But when he heard that Archelaus was reigning in Judea in place of his father Herod, he was afraid to go there. Having been warned in a dream, he withdrew to the district of Galilee, and he went and lived in a town called Nazareth. So was fulfilled what was said through the prophets, that he would be called a Nazarene.

Matthew 2:19-23 NIV

With the loving mercy of our God, a new day from heaven will dawn upon us. It will shine on those who live in darkness, in the shadow of death. It will guide us into the path of peace.

Luke 1:78-79 NCV

So don't be afraid, little flock. For it gives your Father great happiness to give you the Kingdom.

Luke 12:32 NLT

But there shall not a hair of your head perish.

Luke 21:18

And you shall know the truth, and the truth shall make you free.

Therefore, if the Son makes you free, you shall be free indeed.

John 8:32, 36 NKJV

My sheep recognize my voice. I know them, and they follow me. I give them real and eternal life. They are protected from the Destroyer for good. No one can steal them from out of my hand. The Father who put them under my care is so much greater than the Destroyer and Thief. No one could ever get them away from him. I and the Father are one heart and mind."

John 10:27-30 MSG

I have told you these things, so that in me you may have peace. In this world you will have trouble. But take heart! I have overcome the world.

John 16:33 NIV

I do not pray that You should take them out of the world, but that You should keep them from the evil one.

John 17:15 NKJV

The night before Herod was to bring him to trial, Peter was sleeping between two soldiers, bound with two chains. Other soldiers were guarding the door of the jail. Suddenly, an angel of the Lord stood there, and a light shined in the cell. The angel struck Peter on the side and woke him up. "Hurry! Get up!" the angel said. And the chains fell off Peter's hands. Then the angel told him, "Get dressed and put on your sandals." And Peter did. Then the angel said, "Put on your coat and follow me." So Peter followed him out, but he did not know if what the angel was doing was real; he thought he might be seeing a vision. They went past the first and second guards and came to the iron gate that separated them from the city. The gate opened by itself for them, and they went through it. When they had walked down one street, the angel suddenly left him.

Then Peter realized what had happened. He thought, "Now I know that the Lord really sent his angel to me. He rescued me from Herod and from all the things the people thought would happen."

Acts 12:6-11 NCV

One night the Lord spoke to Paul in a vision and told him, "Don't be afraid! Speak out! Don't be silent! For I am with you, and no one will attack and harm you, for many people in this city belong to me."

Acts 18:9-10 NLT

Last night an angel of the God to whom I belong and whom I serve stood beside me and said, 'Do not be afraid, Paul. You must stand trial before Caesar; and God has graciously given you the lives of all who sail with you.' So keep up your courage, men, for I have faith in God that it will happen just as he told me.

Acts 27:23-25 NIV

There is therefore now no condemnation to those who are in Christ Jesus, who do not walk according to the flesh, but according to the Spirit. For the law of the Spirit of life in Christ Jesus has made me free from the law of sin and death.

Romans 8:1-2 NKJV

If God is for us, who can be against us?

Romans 8:31

Don't be intimidated in any way by your enemies. This will be a sign to them that they are going to be destroyed, but that you are going to be saved, even by God himself.

Phillippians 1:28 NLT

Those things were important to me, but now I think they are worth nothing because of Christ.

Not only those things, but I think that all things are worth nothing compared with the greatness of knowing Christ Jesus my Lord. Because of him, I have lost all those things, and now I know they are worthless trash. This allows me to have Christ.

Phillippians 3:7-8 NCV

For he has rescued us from the dominion of darkness and brought us into the kingdom of the Son he loves.

Colossians 1:13 NIV

But the Lord is faithful, who will establish you and guard you from the evil one.

2 Thessalonians 3:3 NKJV

The Lord will rescue me from every evil attack and will bring me safely to his heavenly kingdom. To him be glory for ever and ever. Amen.

2 Timothy 4:18 NIV

God has said, "I will never leave you; I will never abandon you."

So we can be sure when we say, "I will not be afraid, because the Lord is my helper. People can't do anything to me."

Hebrews 13:5-6 NCV

Casting all your anxiety on Him, because He cares for you.

1 Peter 5:7 NASB

Now all glory to God, who is able to keep you from falling away and will bring you with great joy into his glorious presence without a single fault.

All glory to him who alone is God, our Savior through Jesus Christ our Lord. All glory, majesty, power, and authority are his before all time, and in the present, and beyond all time! Amen.

Jude 1:24-25 NLT

Healing Scriptures
Old Testament

He said, "If you will listen carefully to the voice of the Lord your God and do what is right in his sight, obeying his commands and keeping all his decrees, then I will not make you suffer any of the diseases I sent on the Egyptians; for I am the Lord who heals you."

Exodus 15:26 NLT

I, the Lord, am your healer.

Exodus 15:26b NASB

Honor your father and your mother, so that you may live long in the land the Lord your God is giving you.

Exodus 20:12 NIV

So you shall serve the Lord your God, and He will bless your bread and your water. And I will take sickness away from the midst of you.

No one shall suffer miscarriage or be barren in your land; I will fulfill the number of your days.

Exodus 23: 25-26 NKJV

God is not human, that he should lie, not a human being, that he should change his mind. Does he speak and then not act? Does he promise and not fulfill?

Numbers 23:19 NIV

So be careful to obey the commands, rules, and laws I give you today. If you pay attention to these laws and obey them carefully, the LORD your God will keep his agreement and show his love to you, as he promised your ancestors. He will love and bless you. He will make the number of your people grow; he will bless you with children. He will bless your fields with good crops and will give you grain, new wine, and oil. He will bless your herds with calves and your flocks with lambs in the land he promised your ancestors he would give you. You will be blessed more than any other people. Every husband and wife will have children, and all your cattle will have calves. The LORD will take away all disease from you; you will not have the terrible diseases that were in Egypt, but he will give them to all the people who hate you.

Deuteronomy 7:11-15 NCV

I call heaven and earth to witness this day against you that I have set before you life and death, the blessings and the curses; therefore choose life, that you and your descendants may live.

And may love the Lord your God, obey His voice, and cling to Him. For He is your life and the length of your days

Deuteronomy 30:19, 20 AMP

For the joy of the LORD is your strength.

Nehemiah 8:10

Be gracious to me, O LORD, for I am pining away; Heal me, O LORD, for my bones are dismayed.

Psalm 6:2 NASB

He asked you for life, and you gave it to him —length of days, for ever and ever.

Psalm 21:4 NIV

LORD my God, I called to you for help, and you healed me.

Psalm 30:2 NIV

All you who put your hope in the LORD be strong and brave.

Psalm 31:24 NCV

Do you want a long, good life? Then watch your tongue! Keep your lips from lying.

Psalm 34:12-13 TLB

Is anyone crying for help? GOD is listening, ready to rescue you.

If your heart is broken, you'll find God right there; if you're kicked in the gut, he'll help you catch your breath.

Psalm 34:17-18 MSG

People who do what is right may have many problems, but the LORD will solve them all.

He will protect their very bones; not one of them will be broken.

Psalm 34: 19-20 NCV

The LORD sustains them on their sickbed and restores them from their bed of illness.

Psalm 41:3 NIV

God be merciful to us and bless us, and cause His face to shine upon us, *Selah.*

That Your way may be known on earth, Your salvation among all nations.

Psalm 67: 1-2 NKJV

Praise be to the LORD, to God our Savior, who daily bears our burdens.

Psalm 68:19 NIV

Those who live in the shelter of the Most High will find rest in the shadow of the Almighty. This I declare about the LORD: He alone is my refuge, my place of safety; he is my God, and I trust him. For he will rescue you from every trap and protect you from deadly disease.

Psalm 91:1-3 NLT

No evil will conquer you; no plague will come near your home.

For he will order his angels to protect you wherever you go.

They will hold you up with their hands so you won't even hurt your foot on a stone.

You will trample upon lions and cobras; you will crush fierce lions and serpents under your feet!

The LORD says, "I will rescue those who love me. I will protect those who trust in my name.

When they call on me, I will answer; I will be with them in trouble. I will rescue and honor them.

I will reward them with a long life and give them my salvation."

Psalm 91: 10-16 NLT

Bless the LORD, O my soul, and forget not all his benefits:

Who forgiveth all thine iniquities; who healeth all thy diseases;

Who redeemeth thy life from destruction; who crowneth thee with loving kindness and tender mercies;

Who satisfieth thy mouth with good things; so that thy youth is renewed like the eagle's.

Psalm 103: 2-5

He brought them forth also with silver and gold: and there was not one feeble person among their tribes.

Psalm 105:37

He sent his word, and healed them, and delivered them from their destructions.

Psalm 107:20

He settles the childless woman in her home as a happy mother of children. Praise the LORD.

Psalm 113:9 NIV

I shall not die, but live, and declare the works of the LORD.

Psalm 118:17

I will lift up my eyes to the hills from whence comes my help? My help comes from the LORD, who made heaven and earth.

He will not allow your foot to be moved; he who keeps you will not slumber.

Behold, He who keeps Israel shall neither slumber nor sleep.

The LORD is your keeper; the LORD is your shade at your right hand.

The sun shall not strike you by day, nor the moon by night.

The LORD shall preserve you from all evil; he shall preserve your soul.

The LORD shall preserve your going out and your coming in from this time forth, and even forevermore.

Psalm 121:1-8 NKJV

The Lord will perfect that which concerns me.

Psalm 138:8 AMP

He heals the brokenhearted and binds up their wounds [curing their pains and their sorrows].

Psalm 147:3 AMP

My son, do not forget my law, but let your heart keep my commands;

For length of days and long life and peace they will add to you.

Proverbs 3: 1-2 NKJV

Do not be wise in your own eyes; fear the LORD and shun evil.

This will bring health to your body and nourishment to your bones.

Proverbs 3: 7, 8 NIV

With her right hand wisdom offers you a long life, and with her left hand she gives you riches and honor.

Proverbs 3:16 NCV

My son, give attention to my words; incline your ear to my sayings.

Do not let them depart from your eyes; keep them in the midst of your heart;

For they are life to those who find them, and health to all their flesh.

Proverbs 4:20-22 NKJV

Keep my commands and you will live; guard my teachings as the apple of your eye.

Proverbs 7:2 NIV

Wisdom will multiply your days and add years to your life.

Proverbs 9:11 NLT

The mouth of a good person is a deep, life-giving well.

Proverbs 10:11 MSG

The fear of the LORD prolongs life, but the years of the wicked will be shortened.

Proverbs 10:27 NASB

Truly the righteous attain life, but whoever pursues evil finds death.

Proverbs 11:19 NIV

There is one who speaks like the piercings of a sword, but the tongue of the wise promotes health.

Proverbs 12:18 NKJV

In the way of righteousness is life: and in the pathway thereof there is no death.

Proverbs 12:28

A sound heart is life to the body, but envy is rottenness to the bones.

Proverbs 14:30 NKJV

A calm and undisturbed mind and heart are the life and health of the body, but envy, jealousy, and wrath are like rotten-ness of the bones.

Proverbs 14:30 AMP

A wholesome tongue is a tree of life

Proverbs 15:4

Light in a messenger's eyes brings joy to the heart, and good news gives health to the bones.

Proverbs 15:30 NIV

Pleasant words are as an honeycomb, sweet to the soul, and health to the bones.

Proverbs 16:24

Kind words are like honey—enjoyable and healthful.

Proverbs 16:24 TLB

A cheerful disposition is good for your health; gloom and doom leave you bone-tired.

Proverbs 17:22 MSG

Wise words satisfy like a good meal; the right words bring satisfaction.

The tongue can bring death or life; those who love to talk will reap the consequences.

Proverbs 18:20-21 NLT

You will keep in perfect peace those whose minds are steadfast, because they trust in you.

Trust in the LORD forever, for the LORD, the LORD himself, is the Rock eternal.

Isaiah 26:3-4 NIV

For with stammering lips and another tongue will he speak to this people.

To whom he said, This is the rest wherewith ye may cause the weary to rest; and this is the refreshing: yet they would not hear.

Isaiah 28:11-12

People will look to the king for help, and they will truly listen to what he says.

People who are now worried will be able to understand. Those who cannot speak clearly now will then be able to speak clearly and quickly.

Isaiah 32:3-4 NCV

Strengthen ye the weak hands, and confirm the feeble knees.

Isaiah 35:3

Then will the eyes of the blind be opened and the ears of the deaf unstopped.

Isaiah 35:5 NIV

Then will the lame leap like a deer, and the mute tongue shout for joy.

Isaiah 35:6 NIV

He gives strength to the weary and increases the power of the weak.

Even youths grow tired and weary, and young men stumble and fall;

but those who hope in the LORD will renew their strength. They will soar on wings like eagles; they will run and not grow weary, they will walk and not be faint.

Isaiah 40:29-31 NIV

Hear, ye deaf; and look, ye blind, that ye may see.

Isaiah 42:18

But now, thus says the LORD, your Creator, O Jacob, and He who formed you, O Israel, "Do not fear, for I have redeemed you; I have called you by name; you are Mine!

When you pass through the waters, I will be with you; and through the rivers, they will not overflow you. When you walk through the fire, you will not be scorched, nor will the flame burn you.

Isaiah 43:1-2 NASB

Surely He has borne our griefs and carried our sorrows; yet we esteemed Him stricken, smitten by God, and afflicted.

But He was wounded for our transgressions, he was bruised for our iniquities; the chastisement for our peace was upon Him, and by His stripes we are healed.

Isaiah 53:4-5 NKJV

But in that coming day no weapon turned against you will succeed. You will silence every voice raised up to accuse you. These benefits are enjoyed by the servants of the LORD; their vindication will come from me. I, the LORD, have spoken!

Isaiah 54:17 NLT

So shall My word be that goes forth from My mouth; it shall not return to Me void, but it shall accomplish what I please, and it shall prosper in the thing for which I sent it.

Isaiah 55:11 NKJV

"I have seen his ways, but I will heal him; I will lead him and restore comfort to him and to his mourners, creating the praise of the lips. peace, peace to him who is far and to him who is near," says the LORD, "and I will heal him."

Isaiah 57: 18-19 NASB

Then shall your light break forth like the morning, and your healing (your restoration and the power of a new life) shall spring forth speedily; your righteousness (your rightness, your justice, and your right relationship with God) shall go before you [conducting you to peace and prosperity], and the glory of the Lord shall be your rear guard.

Isaiah 58:8 AMP

For I am watching to see that my word is fulfilled.

Jeremiah 1:12

"My wayward children," says the LORD, "come back to me, and I will heal your wayward hearts."

Jeremiah 3:22 NLT

Heal me, O LORD, and I shall be healed; save me, and I shall be saved: for thou art my praise.

Jeremiah 17:14

For I know the plans I have for you," declares the LORD, "plans to prosper you and not
to harm you, plans to give you hope and a future."

Jeremiah 29:11 NIV

"I will bring back your health and heal your injuries," says the LORD.

Jeremiah 30:17 NCV

Nevertheless, I will bring health and healing to it; I will heal my people and will let them enjoy abundant peace and security.

Jeremiah 33:6 NIV

But I came by and saw you there, helplessly kicking about in your own blood. As you lay there, I said, 'Live!'

Ezekiel 16:6 NLT

I will heal their backsliding, I will love them freely: for mine anger is turned away from him.

Hosea 14:4

Let the weak say, I am strong.

Joel 3:10

For I am the LORD, I change not.

Malachi 3:6

"But for you who revere my name, the sun of righteousness will rise with healing in its rays. And you will go out and frolic like well-fed calves.

Then you will trample on the wicked; they will be ashes under the soles of your feet on the day when I act," says the LORD Almighty.

Malachi 4:2-3 NIV

HEALING SCRIPTURES
NEW TESTAMENT

Jesus went throughout Galilee, teaching in their synagogues, proclaiming the good news of the kingdom, and healing every disease and sickness among the people.

News about him spread all over Syria, and people brought to him all who were ill with various diseases, those suffering severe pain, the demon-possessed, those having seizures, and the paralyzed; and he healed them.

Matthew 4:23-24 NIV

And, behold, there came a leper and worshipped him, saying, Lord, if thou wilt, thou canst make me clean.

And Jesus put forth his hand, and touched him, saying, I will; be thou clean. And immediately his leprosy was cleansed.

Matthew 8:2-3

When Jesus returned to Capernaum, a Roman officer came and pleaded with him, "Lord, my young servant lies in bed, paralyzed and in terrible pain."

Jesus said, "I will come and heal him."

But the officer said, "Lord, I am not worthy to have you come into my home. Just say the word from where you are, and my servant will be healed.

I know this because I am under the authority of my superior officers, and I have authority over my soldiers. I only need to say, 'Go,' and they go, or 'Come,' and they come. And if I say to my slaves, 'Do this,' they do it."

When Jesus heard this, he was amazed. Turning to those who were following him, he said, "I tell you the truth, I haven't seen faith like this in all Israel!"

Then Jesus said to the Roman officer, "Go back home. Because you believed, it has happened." And the young servant was healed that same hour.

Matthew 8:5-10, 13 NLT

Then on coming into Peter's house Jesus saw that Peter's mother-in-law had been put to bed with a high fever. He touched her hand and the fever left her. And then she got up and began to see to their neeeds.

Matthew 8:14-15 Phillips

When evening had come, they brought to Him many who were demon-possessed. And He cast out the spirits with a word, and healed all who were sick,

That it might be fulfilled which was spoken by Isaiah the prophet, saying: "He Himself took our infirmities and bore our sicknesses."

Matthew 8:16-17 NKJV

Some men brought a sick man to him. The man could not move his arms or legs. He was lying on a bed. Jesus saw that they believed he would be healed. So he said to the sick man, `My son, be glad! The wrong things you have done are forgiven.'

The man got up and went home.

Matthew 9:2,7 WE

As Jesus went on from there, two blind men followed him, calling out, "Have mercy on us, Son of David!"

When he had gone indoors, the blind men came to him, and he asked them, "Do you believe that I am able to do this?" "Yes, Lord," they replied.

Then he touched their eyes and said; "According to your faith let it be done to you";

and their sight was restored. Jesus warned them sternly, "See that no one knows about this."

But they went out and spread the news about him all over that region.

Matthew 9:27-31 NIV

When the two men were leaving, some people brought another man to Jesus. This man could not talk because he had a demon in him.

After Jesus forced the demon to leave the man, he was able to speak.

Matthew 9:32,33 NCV

And Jesus went about all the cities and villages, teaching in their synagogues, and preaching the gospel of the kingdom, and healing every sickness and every disease among the people.

Matthew 9:35

Jesus called his twelve disciples to him and gave them authority to drive out impure spirits and to heal every disease and sickness.

"As you go, proclaim this message: 'The kingdom of heaven has come near'.

Heal the sick, raise the dead, cleanse those who have leprosy, drive out demons. Freely you have received; freely give."

Matthew 10: 1,7,8 NIV

Jesus gave them this reply, "Go and tell John what you see and hear—that blind men are recovering their sight, cripples are walking, lepers being healed, the deaf hearing, the dead being brought to life and the good news is being given to those in need."

Matthew 11: 4-5 Phillips

Are you tired? Worn out? Burned out on religion? Come to me. Get away with me and you'll recover your life. I'll show you how to take a real rest. Walk with me and work with me—watch how I do it. Learn the unforced rhythms of grace. I won't lay anything heavy or ill-fitting on you. Keep company with me and you'll learn to live freely and lightly.

Matthew 11:28-30 MSG

Going on from that place, he went into their synagogue, and a man with a shriveled hand was there. Looking for a rea son to bring charges against Jesus, they asked him, "Is it lawful to heal on the Sabbath?"

He said to them, "If any of you has a sheep and it falls into a pit on the Sabbath, will you not take hold of it and lift it out?

How much more valuable is a person than a sheep! Therefore it is lawful to do good on the Sabbath."

Then he said to the man, "Stretch out your hand." So he stretched it out and it was completely restored, just as sound as the other.

Matthew 12:9-13 NIV

Many people followed him. He healed all the sick among them.

Matthew 12:15 NLT

Then one was brought to Him who was demon-possessed, blind and mute; and He healed him, so that the blind and mute man both spoke and saw.

Matthew 12:22 NKJV

And Jesus went forth, and saw a great multitude, and was moved with compassion toward them, and he healed their sick.

Matthew 14:14

When they had crossed over, they came to the land of Gennesaret.

And when the men of that place recognized Him, they sent out into all that surrounding region, brought to Him all who were sick, and begged Him that they might only touch the hem of His garment. And as many as touched it were made perfectly well.

Matthew 14:34-36 NKJV

A Gentile woman who lived there came to him, pleading, "Have mercy on me, O Lord, Son of David! For my daughter is possessed by a demon that torments her severely."

But Jesus gave her no reply, not even a word. Then his disciples urged him to send her away. "Tell her to go away," they said. "She is bothering us with all her begging."

Then Jesus said to the woman, "I was sent only to help God's lost sheep—the people of Israel."

But she came and worshiped him, pleading again, "Lord, help me!"

Jesus responded, "It isn't right to take food from the children and throw it to the dogs."

She replied, "That's true, Lord, but even dogs are allowed to eat the scraps that fall beneath their masters' table."

"Dear woman," Jesus said to her, "your faith is great. Your request is granted." And her daughter was instantly healed.

Matthew 15:22-28 NLT

After leaving there, Jesus went along the shore of Lake Galilee. He went up on a hill and sat there.

Great crowds came to Jesus, bringing with them the lame, the blind, the crippled, those who could not speak, and many others. They put them at Jesus' feet, and he healed them.

The crowd was amazed when they saw that people who could not speak before were now able to speak. The crippled were made strong.

The lame could walk, and the blind could see. And they praised the God of Israel for this.

Matthew 15:29-31 NCV

When they returned to the crowds again a man came and knelt in front of Jesus. "Lord, do have pity on my son," he said, "for he is a lunatic and is in a terrible state. He is always falling into the fire or into the water. I did bring him to your disciples but they couldn't cure him."

You really are an unbelieving and difficult people," Jesus returned. "How long must I be with you, and how long must I put up with you? Bring him here to me!"

Then Jesus reprimanded the evil spirit and it went out of the boy, who was cured from that moment.

Afterwards the disciples approached Jesus privately and asked, "Why weren't we able to get rid of it?"

"Because you have so little faith," replied Jesus. "I assure you that if you have as much faith as a grain of mustard-seed you can say to this hill, 'Up you get and move over there!' and it will move—you will find nothing is impossible. However, this kind does not go out except by prayer and fasting."

Matthew 17:14-21 Phillips

"Truly I tell you, whatever you bind on earth will be bound in heaven, and whatever you loose on earth will be loosed in heaven.

Again, truly I tell you that if two of you on earth agree about anything they ask for, it will be done for them by my Father in heaven.

For where two or three gather in my name, there am I with them."

Matthew 18:18-20 NIV

After Jesus said all these things, he left Galilee and went into the area of Judea on the other side of the Jordan River.

Large crowds followed him, and he healed them there.

Matthew 19:1-2 NCV

And as they departed from Jericho, a great multitude followed him. And, behold, two blind men sitting by the way side, when they heard that Jesus passed by, cried out, saying, Have mercy on us, O Lord, thou son of David.

And the multitude rebuked them, because they should hold their peace: but they cried the more, saying, Have mercy on us, O Lord, thou son of David.

And Jesus stood still, and called them, and said, What will ye that I shall do unto you?

They say unto him, Lord, that our eyes may be opened.

So Jesus had compassion on them, and touched their eyes: and immediately their eyes received sight, and they followed him.

Matthew 20:29-34

And the blind and the lame came to him in the temple; and he healed them.

Matthew 21:14

Simon's mother-in-law was in bed with a fever, and they immediately told Jesus about her.

So he went to her, took her hand and helped her up. The fever left her and she began to wait on them.

Mark 1:30-31 NIV

When evening came, after the sun had set, they began bringing to Him all who were ill and those who were demon-possessed.

And the whole city had gathered at the door.

And He healed many who were ill with various diseases, and cast out many demons; and He was not permitting the demons to speak, because they knew who He was.

Mark 1:32-34 NASB

When Jesus returned to Capernaum several days later, the news spread quickly that he was back home.

Soon the house where he was staying was so packed with visitors that there was no more room, even outside the door. While he was preaching God's word to them, four men arrived carrying a paralyzed man on a mat.

They couldn't bring him to Jesus because of the crowd, so

they dug a hole through the roof above his head. Then they lowered the man on his mat, right down in front of Jesus.

Seeing their faith, Jesus said to the paralyzed man, "My child, your sins are forgiven."

But some of the teachers of religious law who were sitting there thought to themselves,

"What is he saying? This is blasphemy! Only God can forgive sins!"

Jesus knew immediately what they were thinking, so he asked them, "Why do you question this in your hearts?

Is it easier to say to the paralyzed man 'Your sins are forgiven,' or 'Stand up, pick up your mat, and walk'?

So I will prove to you that the Son of Man has the authority on earth to forgive sins." Then Jesus turned to the paralyzed man and said,

"Stand up, pick up your mat, and go home!"

And the man jumped up, grabbed his mat, and walked out through the stunned onlookers.

They were all amazed and praised God, exclaiming, "We've never seen anything like this before!"

Mark 2:1-12 NLT

Jesus went into the meeting house again. A man was there whose right hand was thin and weak.

The Pharisees watched Jesus to see if he would heal the man on the Sabbath day. They wanted to find something wrong about Jesus.

He spoke to the man whose hand was thin and weak. He said, `Stand here.'

Then he spoke to the Pharisees. He said, `Is it right to do good things on the Sabbath day or to do wrong things? Is it right to heal people so they will live, or to let them die?' But the Pharisees said nothing.

Jesus was angry as he looked at them. And he was sad that their hearts were so hard. Then he said to the man, `Hold out your hand.' The man did so, and it was made well like the other hand.

Mark 3:1-5 WE

So they arrived on the other side of the lake in the country of the Gerasenes. As Jesus was getting out of the boat, a man in the grip of an evil spirit rushed to meet him from among the tombs where he was living. It was no longer possible for any human being to restrain him even with a chain. Indeed he had frequently been secured with fetters and lengths of chain, but he had simply snapped the chains and broken the fetters in pieces. No one could do anything with him. All through the night as well as in the day-time he screamed among the tombs and on the hill-side, and cut himself with stones. Now, as soon as he saw Jesus in the distance, he ran and knelt before him, yelling at the top of his voice, "What have you got to do with me, Jesus, Son of the most high God? For God's sake, don't torture me!"

For Jesus had already said, "Come out of this man, you evil spirit!"

Then he asked him, "What is your name?" "My name is legion," he replied, "for there are many of us." Then he begged and prayed him not to send "them" out of the country.

A large herd of pigs was grazing there on the hill-side, and the evil spirits implored him, "Send us over to the pigs and we'll get into them!"

So Jesus allowed them to do this, and they came out of the man, and made off and went into the pigs. The whole herd of about two thousand stampeded down the cliff into the lake and was drowned. The swineherds took to their heels and spread their story in the city and all over the countryside. Then the people came to see what had happened. As they approached

Jesus, they saw the man who had been devil-possessed sitting there properly clothed and perfectly sane—the same man who had been possessed by "legion"—and they were really frightened. Those who had seen the incident told them what had happened to the devil-possessed man and about the disaster to the pigs. Then they began to implore Jesus to leave their district. As he was embarking on the small boat, the man who had been possessed begged that he might go with him. But Jesus would not allow this. "Go home to your own people," he told him, "And tell them what the Lord has done for you, and how kind he has been to you!"

So the man went off and began to spread throughout the Ten Towns the story of what Jesus had done for him. And they were all simply amazed.

Mark 5:1-20 Phillips

And a certain woman, which had an issue of blood twelve years,

and had suffered many things of many physicians, and had spent all that she had, and was nothing bettered, but rather grew worse, when she had heard of Jesus, came in the press behind, and touched his garment.

For she said, If I may touch but his clothes, I shall be whole.

And straightway the fountain of her blood was dried up; and she felt in her body that she was healed of that plague.

And Jesus, immediately knowing in himself that virtue had gone out of him, turned him about in the press, and said, Who touched my clothes?

Mark 5:25-30

They beached the boat at Gennesaret and tied up at the landing. As soon as they got out of the boat, word got around fast. People ran this way and that, bringing their sick on stretchers to where they heard he was.

Wherever he went, village or town or country crossroads, they brought their sick to the marketplace and begged him to let them touch the edge of his coat—that's all. And whoever touched him became well.

Mark 6:53-56 MSG

Then Jesus left the area around Tyre and went through Sidon to Lake Galilee, to the area of the Ten Towns.

While he was there, some people brought a man to him who was deaf and could not talk plainly. The people begged Jesus to put his hand on the man to heal him.

Jesus led the man away from the crowd, by himself. He put

his fingers in the man's ears and then spit and touched the man's tongue.

Looking up to heaven, he sighed and said to the man, "Ephphatha!" (This means, "Be opened.")

Instantly the man was able to hear and to use his tongue so that he spoke clearly.

Mark 7:31-35 NCV

They came to Bethsaida, and some people brought a blind man and begged Jesus to touch him.

He took the blind man by the hand and led him outside the village. When he had spit on the man's eyes and put his hands on him, Jesus asked, "Do you see anything?"

He looked up and said, "I see people; they look like trees walking around."

Once more Jesus put his hands on the man's eyes. Then his eyes were opened, his sight was restored, and he saw everything clearly.

Mark 8:22-25 NIV

Then one of the crowd answered and said, "Teacher, I brought You my son, who has a mute spirit.

And wherever it seizes him, it throws him down; he foams at

the mouth, gnashes his teeth, and becomes rigid. So I spoke to Your disciples, that they should cast it out, but they could not."

He answered him and said, "O faithless generation, how long shall I be with you? How long shall I bear with you? Bring him to Me."

Then they brought him to Him. And when he saw Him, immediately the spirit convulsed him, and he fell on the ground and wallowed, foaming at the mouth.

So He asked his father, "How long has this been happening to him?" And he said, "From childhood.

And often he has thrown him both into the fire and into the water to destroy him. But if You can do anything, have compassion on us and help us."

Jesus said to him, "If you can believe, all things are possible to him who believes."

Immediately the father of the child cried out and said with tears, "Lord, I believe; help my unbelief!"

When Jesus saw that the people came running together, He rebuked the unclean spirit, saying to it: "Deaf and dumb spirit, I command you, come out of him and enter him no more!"

Then the spirit cried out, convulsed him greatly, and came

out of him. And he became as one dead, so that many said, "He is dead."

But Jesus took him by the hand and lifted him up, and he arose.

And when He had come into the house, His disciples asked Him privately, "Why could we not cast it out?"

So He said to them, "This kind can come out by nothing but prayer and fasting."

Mark 9:17-29 NKJV

Then they came to Jericho. As Jesus and his disciples, together with a large crowd, were leaving the city, a blind man, Bartimaeus (which means "son of Timaeus"), was sitting by the roadside begging.

When he heard that it was Jesus of Nazareth, he began to shout, "Jesus, Son of David, have mercy on me!"

Many rebuked him and told him to be quiet, but he shouted all the more, "Son of David, have mercy on me!"

Jesus stopped and said, "Call him."

So they called to the blind man, "Cheer up! On your feet! He's calling you."

Throwing his cloak aside, he jumped to his feet and came to Jesus.

"What do you want me to do for you?' Jesus asked him. The blind man said, "Rabbi, I want to see."

"Go," said Jesus, "your faith has healed you." Immediately he received his sight and followed Jesus along the road.

Mark 10:46-52 NIV

Jesus answered, "Have faith in God.

I tell you the truth, you can say to this mountain, 'Go, fall into the sea.' And if you have no doubts in your mind and believe that what you say will happen, God will do it for you.

So I tell you to believe that you have received the things you ask for in prayer, and God will give them to you.

When you are praying, if you are angry with someone, forgive him so that your Father in heaven will also forgive your sins.

Mark 11:22-25 NCV

I tell you the truth, you can say to this mountain, 'May you be lifted up and thrown into the sea,' and it will happen. But you must really believe it will happen and have no doubt in your heart.

I tell you, you can pray for anything, and if you believe that you've received it, it will be yours.

Mark 11:23-24 NLT

These signs will be with those who believe. They will drive bad spirits out of people by using my name. They will speak new languages.

They will take up snakes. If they drink poison, it will not make them sick. They will put their hands on sick people and sick people will get well again.

Mark 16:17-18 WE

For with God nothing shall be impossible.

Luke 1:37

For no promise of God can fail to be fulfilled.

Luke 1:37 Phillips

The Spirit of the Lord is upon me, because he hath anointed me to preach the gospel to the poor; he hath sent me to heal the brokenhearted, to preach deliverance to the captives, and recovering of sight to the blind, to set at liberty them that are bruised, to preach the acceptable year of the Lord.

Luke 4:18-19

After leaving the synagogue that day, Jesus went to Simon's home, where he found Simon's mother-in-law very sick with a high fever. "Please heal her," everyone begged.

Standing at her bedside, he rebuked the fever, and it left her. And she got up at once and prepared a meal for them.

Luke 4:38-29 NLT

When the sun went down, the people brought those who were sick to Jesus. Putting his hands on each sick person, he healed every one of them.

Luke 4:40 NCV

Then, as the sun was setting, all those who had friends suffering from every kind of disease brought them to Jesus and he laid his hands on each one of them separately and healed them. Evil spirits came out of many of these people, shouting, "You are the Son of God!" But he spoke sharply to them and would not allow them to say any more, for they knew perfectly well that he was Christ.

Luke 4:40-41 Phillips

In one of the villages, Jesus met a man with an advanced case of leprosy. When the man saw Jesus, he bowed with his face to the ground, begging to be healed. "Lord," he said, "if you are willing, you can heal me and make me clean."

Jesus reached out and touched him. "I am willing," he said. "Be healed!" And instantly the leprosy disappeared.

Then Jesus instructed him not to tell anyone what had happened. He said, "Go to the priest and let him examine you. Take along the offering required in the law of Moses for those who have been healed of leprosy. This will be a public testimony that you have been cleansed."

But despite Jesus' instructions, the report of his power spread even faster, and vast crowds came to hear him preach and to be healed of their diseases.

Luke 5:12-15 NLT

Jesus realised what was going on in their minds and spoke straight to them.

"Why must you argue like this in your minds? Which do you suppose is easier—to say, 'Your sins are forgiven' or to say, 'Get up and walk'? But to make you realise that the Son of Man has full authority on earth to forgive sins—I tell you," he said to the man who was paralysed, "get up, pick up your bed and go home!"

Instantly the man sprang to his feet before their eyes, picked up the bedding on which he used to lie, and went off home, praising God. Sheer amazement gripped every man present, and they praised God and said in awed voices, "We have seen incredible things today."

Luke 5:22-26 Phillips

And it came to pass also on another sabbath, that he entered into the synagogue and taught: and there was a man whose right hand was withered.

And the scribes and Pharisees watched him, whether he would heal on the sabbath day; that they might find an accusation against him.

But he knew their thoughts, and said to the man which had the withered hand, Rise up, and stand forth in the midst. And he arose and stood forth.

Then said Jesus unto them, I will ask you one thing; Is it lawful on the sabbath days to do good, or to do evil? to save life, or to destroy it?

And looking round about upon them all, he said unto the

man, Stretch forth thy hand. And he did so: and his hand was restored whole as the other.

Luke 6:6-10

He went down with them and stood on a level place. A large crowd of his disciples was there and a great number of people from all over Judea, from Jerusalem, and from the coastal region around Tyre and Sidon,

who had come to hear him and to be healed of their diseases. Those troubled by impure spirits were cured,

and the people all tried to touch him, because power was coming from him and healing them all.

Luke 6:17-19 NIV

When Jesus finished saying all these things to the people, he went to Capernaum.

There was an army officer who had a servant who was very important to him. The servant was so sick he was nearly dead.

When the officer heard about Jesus, he sent some Jewish elders to him to ask Jesus to come and heal his servant.

The men went to Jesus and begged him, saying, "This officer is worthy of your help.

He loves our people, and he built us a synagogue."

So Jesus went with the men. He was getting near the officer's house when the officer sent friends to say, "Lord, don't trouble yourself, because I am not worthy to have you come into my house.

That is why I did not come to you myself. But you only need to command it, and my servant will be healed.

"I, too, am a man under the authority of others, and I have soldiers under my command. I tell one soldier, 'Go,' and he goes. I tell another soldier, 'Come,' and he comes. I say to my servant, 'Do this,' and my servant does it."

When Jesus heard this, he was amazed. Turning to the crowd that was following him, he said, "I tell you, this is the greatest faith I have found anywhere, even in Israel."

Those who had been sent to Jesus went back to the house where they found the servant in good health.

Luke 7:1-10 NCV

Soon afterward Jesus went with his disciples to the village of Nain, and a large crowd followed him.

A funeral procession was coming out as he approached the village gate. The young man who had died was a widow's only son, and a large crowd from the village was with her.

When the Lord saw her, his heart overflowed with

compassion. "Don't cry!" he said.

Then he walked over to the coffin and touched it, and the bearers stopped. "Young man," he said, "I tell you, get up."

Then the dead boy sat up and began to talk! And Jesus gave him back to his mother.

Luke 7:11-15 NLT

When the men came to Jesus, they said, "John the Baptist sent us to you to ask, 'Are you the one who is to come, or should we expect someone else?'"

At that very time Jesus cured many who had diseases, sicknesses and evil spirits, and gave sight to many who were blind.

So he replied to the messengers, "Go back and report to John what you have seen and heard: The blind receive sight, the lame walk, those who have leprosy are cleansed, the deaf hear, the dead are raised, and the good news is proclaimed to the poor.

Blessed is anyone who does not stumble on account of me."

Luke 7:20-23 NIV

A woman was in the crowd who had been bleeding for twelve years, but no one was able to heal her.

She came up behind Jesus and touched the edge of his coat, and instantly her bleeding stopped.

Then Jesus said, "Who touched me?"

When all the people said they had not touched him, Peter said, "Master, the people are all around you and are pushing against you."

But Jesus said, "Someone did touch me, because I felt power go out from me."

When the woman saw she could not hide, she came forward, shaking, and fell down before Jesus. While all the people listened, she told why she had touched him and how she had been in-stantly healed.

Jesus said to her, "Dear woman, you are made well because you believed. Go in peace."

Luke 8:43-48 NCV

While he was still speaking to her, a messenger arrived from the Jairus' home with the news that the little girl was dead. "She's gone," he told her father; "there's no use troubling the Teacher now."

But when Jesus heard what had happened, he said to the father, "Don't be afraid! Just trust me, and she'll be all right."

When they arrived at the house Jesus wouldn't let anyone into the room except Peter, James, John and the little girl's father and mother.

The home was filled with mourning people, but he said, "Stop the weeping! She isn't dead; she is only asleep!" This brought scoffing and laughter, for they all knew she was dead.

Then he took her by the hand and called, "Get up, little girl!" And at that moment her life returned and she jumped up! "Give her something to eat!" he said. Her parents were overcome with happiness, but Jesus insisted that they not tell anyone the details of what had happened.

Luke 8:49-56 TLB

Then he called his twelve disciples together, and gave them power and authority over all devils, and to cure diseases.

And he sent them to preach the kingdom of God, and to heal the sick.

And they departed, and went through the towns, preaching the gospel, and healing every where.

Luke 9: 1-2,6

But the crowds learned about it and followed him. He welcomed them and spoke to them about the kingdom of God, and healed those who needed healing.

Luke 9:11 NIV

Behold, I give you the authority to trample on serpents and scorpions, and over all the power of the enemy, and nothing shall by any means hurt you.

Luke 10:19 NKJV

And a woman was there who had been crippled by a spirit for eighteen years. She was bent over and could not straighten up at all.

When Jesus saw her, he called her forward and said to her, "Woman, you are set free from your infirmity."

Then he put his hands on her, and immediately she straightened up and praised God.

Indignant because Jesus had healed on the Sabbath, the synagogue leader said to the people, "There are six days for work. So come and be healed on those days, not on the Sabbath."

The Lord answered him, "You hypocrites! Doesn't each of you on the Sabbath untie your ox or donkey from the stall and lead it out to give it water?

Then should not this woman, a daughter of Abraham, whom Satan has kept bound for eighteen long years, be set free on the Sabbath day from what bound her?"

When he said this, all his opponents were humiliated, but the people were delighted with all the wonderful things he was doing.

Luke 13:11-17 NIV

One Sabbath day Jesus went to eat dinner in the home of a leader of the Pharisees, and the people were watching him closely.

There was a man there whose arms and legs were swollen.

Jesus asked the Pharisees and experts in religious law, "Is it permitted in the law to heal people on the Sabbath day, or not?"

When they refused to answer, Jesus touched the sick man and healed him and sent him away.

Luke 14:1-4 NLT

And it came to pass, as he went to Jerusalem, that he passed through the midst of Samaria and Galilee.

And as he entered into a certain village, there met him ten men that were lepers, which stood afar off:

And they lifted up their voices, and said, Jesus, Master, have mercy on us.

And when he saw them, he said unto them, Go shew yourselves unto the priests. And it came to pass, that, as they went, they were cleansed.

And one of them, when he saw that he was healed, turned back, and with a loud voice glorified God,

and fell down on his face at his feet, giving him thanks: and he was a Samaritan.

And Jesus answering said, Were there not ten cleansed? but where are the nine?

There are not found that returned to give glory to God, save this stranger.

And he said unto him, Arise, go thy way: thy faith hath made thee whole.

Luke 17:11-19

Then, as he was approaching Jericho, it happened that there was a blind man sitting by the roadside, begging. He heard the crowd passing and enquired what it was all about.

And they told him, "Jesus the man from Nazareth is going past you." So he shouted out, "Jesus, Son of David, have pity on me!"

Those who were in front tried to hush his cries. But that made him call out all the more, "Son of David, have pity on me!"

So Jesus stood quite still and ordered the man to be brought to him. And when he was quite close, he said to him, "What do you want me to do for you?" "Lord, make me see again," he cried.

"You can see again! Your faith has cured you," returned Jesus. And his sight was restored at once, and he followed Jesus, praising God. All the people who saw it thanked God too.

Luke 18:35-43 Phillips

When those with him saw what was happening, they said, "Master, shall we fight?" One of them took a swing at the Chief Priest's servant and cut off his right ear.

Jesus said, "Let them be. Even in this." Then, touching the servant's ear, he healed him.

Luke 22:49-51 Message

So Jesus came again to Cana of Galilee where He had made the water wine. And there was a certain nobleman whose son was sick at Capernaum.

When he heard that Jesus had come out of Judea into Galilee, he went to Him and implored Him to come down and heal his son, for he was at the point of death.

Then Jesus said to him, "Unless you people see signs and wonders, you will by no means believe."

The nobleman said to Him, "Sir, come down before my child dies!"

Jesus said to him, "Go your way; your son lives." So the man believed the word that Jesus spoke to him, and he went his way.

And as he was now going down, his servants met him and told him, saying, "Your son lives!"

Then he inquired of them the hour when he got better. And they said to him, "Yesterday at the seventh hour the fever left him."

So the father knew that it was at the same hour in which Jesus said to him, "Your son lives." And he himself believed, and his whole household.

John 4:46-53 NKJV

Jesus saith unto him, Rise, take up thy bed, and walk.
And immediately the man was made whole, and took up his bed, and walked: and on the same day was the sabbath.

John 5:8-9

The Spirit alone gives eternal life. Human effort accomplishes nothing. And the very words I have spoken to you are spirit and life.

John 6:63 NLT

And as Jesus passed by, he saw a man which was blind from his birth.

And his disciples asked him, saying, Master, who did sin, this man, or his parents, that he was born blind?

Jesus answered, Neither hath this man sinned, nor his parents: but that the works of God should be made manifest in him.

I must work the works of him that sent me, while it is day: the night cometh, when no man can work.

As long as I am in the world, I am the light of the world.

When he had thus spoken, he spat on the ground, and made clay of the spittle, and he anointed the eyes of the blind man with the clay,

and said unto him, Go, wash in the pool of Siloam, (which is by interpretation, Sent.) He went his way therefore, and washed, and came seeing.

The neighbours therefore, and they which before had seen him that he was blind, said,

Is not this he that sat and begged?

Some said, This is he: others said, He is like him: but he said, I am he.

Therefore said they unto him, How were thine eyes opened?

He answered and said, A man that is called Jesus made clay, and anointed mine eyes, and said unto me, Go to the pool of Siloam, and wash: and I went and washed, and I received sight.

John 9:1-11

The thief comes only in order to steal and kill and destroy. I came that they may have and enjoy life, and have it in abundance (to the full, till it overflows).

John 10:10 AMP

Now a man named Lazarus was sick. He was from Bethany, the village of Mary and her sister Martha.

(This Mary, whose brother Lazarus now lay sick, was the same one who poured perfume on the Lord and wiped his feet with her hair.)

So the sisters sent word to Jesus, "Lord, the one you love is sick."

When he heard this, Jesus said, "This sickness will not end in death. No, it is for God's glory so that God's Son may be glorified through it."

Now Jesus loved Martha and her sister and Lazarus.

So when he heard that Lazarus was sick, he stayed where he was two more days, and then he said to his disciples, "Let us go back to Judea."

"But Rabbi," they said, "a short while ago the Jews there tried to stone you, and yet you are going back?"

Jesus answered, "Are there not twelve hours of daylight? Anyone who walks in the daytime will not stumble, for they see by this world's light.

It is when a person walks at night that they stumble, for they have no light."

After he had said this, he went on to tell them, "Our friend Lazarus has fallen asleep; but I am going there to wake him up."

His disciples replied, "Lord, if he sleeps, he will get better."

Jesus had been speaking of his death, but his disciples thought he meant natural sleep.

So then he told them plainly, "Lazarus is dead,

and for your sake I am glad I was not there, so that you may believe. But let us go to him."

Then Thomas (also known as Didymus) said to the rest of the disciples, "Let us also go, that we may die with him."

On his arrival, Jesus found that Lazarus had already been in the tomb for four days.

Now Bethany was less than two miles from Jerusalem, and many Jews had come to Martha and Mary to comfort them in the loss of their brother.

When Martha heard that Jesus was coming, she went out to meet him, but Mary stayed at home.

"Lord," Martha said to Jesus, "if you had been here, my brother would not have died.

But I know that even now God will give you whatever you ask."

Jesus said to her, "Your brother will rise again."

Martha answered, "I know he will rise again in the resurrection at the last day."

Jesus said to her, "I am the resurrection and the life. The one who believes in me will live, even though they die;

and whoever lives by believing in me will never die. Do you believe this?"

"Yes, Lord," she replied, "I believe that you are the Messiah, the

Son of God, who is to come into the world."

After she had said this, she went back and called her sister Mary aside. "The Teacher is here," she said, "and is asking for you."

When Mary heard this, she got up quickly and went to him.

Now Jesus had not yet entered the village, but was still at the place where Martha had met him.

When the Jews who had been with Mary in the house, comforting her, noticed how quickly she got up and went out, they followed her, supposing she was going to the tomb to mourn there.

When Mary reached the place where Jesus was and saw him, she fell at his feet and said, "Lord, if you had been here, my brother would not have died."

When Jesus saw her weeping, and the Jews who had come along with her also weeping, he was deeply moved in spirit and troubled.

"Where have you laid him?" he asked. "Come and see, Lord," they replied.

Jesus wept.

Then the Jews said, "See how he loved him!"

But some of them said, "Could not he who opened the eyes of the blind man have kept this man from dying?"

Jesus, once more deeply moved, came to the tomb. It was a cave with a stone laid across the entrance.

"Take away the stone," he said.

"But, Lord," said Martha, the sister of the dead man, "by this time there is a bad odor, for he has been there four days."

Then Jesus said, "Did I not tell you that if you believe, you will see the glory of God?"

So they took away the stone. Then Jesus looked up and said, "Father, I thank you that you have heard me. I knew that you always hear me, but I said this for the benefit of the people standing here, that they may believe that you sent me."

When he had said this, Jesus called in a loud voice, "Lazarus, come out!"

The dead man came out, his hands and feet wrapped with strips of linen, and a cloth around his face. Jesus said to them, "Take off the grave clothes and let him go."

John 11:1-44 NIV

And if you ask for anything in my name, I will do it for you so that the Father's glory will be shown through the Son.

If you ask me for anything in my name, I will do it.

John 14: 13-14 NCV

If you abide in Me, and My words abide in you, ask whatever you wish, and it will be done for you.

John 15:7 NASB

In that day you will not question Me about anything. Truly, truly, I say to you, if you ask the Father for anything in My name, He will give it to you.

Until now you have asked for nothing in My name; ask and you will receive, so that your joy may be made full.

John 16: 23-24 NASB

Now Peter and John were going up to the temple at the ninth hour, the hour of prayer.

And a man who had been lame from his mother's womb was being carried along, whom they used to set down every day at the gate of the temple which is called Beautiful, in order to beg alms of those who were entering the temple.

When he saw Peter and John about to go into the temple, he began asking to receive alms.

But Peter, along with John, fixed his gaze on him and said, "Look at us!"

And he began to give them his attention, expecting to receive something from them.

But Peter said, "I do not possess silver and gold, but what I do have I give to you: In the name of Jesus Christ the Nazarene— walk!"

And seizing him by the right hand, he raised him up; and

immediately his feet and his ankles were strengthened.

With a leap he stood upright and began to walk; and he entered the temple with them, walking and leaping and praising God.

And on the basis of faith in His name, it is the name of Jesus which has strengthened this man whom you see and know; and the faith which comes through Him has given him this perfect health in the presence of you all.

Acts 3:1-8, 16 NASB

Then Peter, filled with the Holy Spirit, said to them: "Rulers and elders of the people!

If we are being called to account today for an act of kindness shown to a man who was lame and are being asked how he was healed,

then know this, you and all the people of Israel: It is by the name of Jesus Christ of Nazareth, whom you crucified but whom God raised from the dead, that this man stands before you healed."

Acts. 4:8-10 NIV

And by the hands of the apostles were many signs and wonders wrought among the people; (and they were all with one accord in Solomon's porch.

And of the rest durst no man join himself to them: but the people magnified them.

And believers were the more added to the Lord, multitudes both of men and women.)

Insomuch that they brought forth the sick into the streets, and laid them on beds and couches, that at the least the shadow of Peter passing by might overshadow some of them.

There came also a multitude out of the cities round about unto Jerusalem, bringing sick folks, and them which were vexed with

unclean spirits: and they were healed every one.

Acts 5:12-16

And Stephen, full of faith and power, did great wonders and miracles among the people.

Acts 6:8

Philip, for example, went to the city of Samaria and told the people there about the Messiah.

Crowds listened intently to Philip because they were eager to hear his message and see the miraculous signs he did.

Many evil spirits were cast out, screaming as they left their victims. And many who had been paralyzed or lame were healed.

So there was great joy in that city.

Acts 8:5-8 NLT

Now it happened that Peter, in the course of travelling about among them all, came to God's people living at Lydda. There he found a man called Aeneas who had been bed-ridden for eight years through paralysis. Peter said to him "Aeneas, Jesus Christ heals you! Get up and make your bed."

He got to his feet at once. And all those who lived in Lydda and Sharon saw him and turned to the Lord.

Acts 9:32-35 Phillips

How God anointed Jesus of Nazareth with the Holy Ghost and with power: who went about doing good, and healing all that were oppressed of the devil; for God was with him.

Acts 10:38

In Lystra there sat a man who was lame. He had been that way from birth and had never walked.

He listened to Paul as he was speaking. Paul looked directly at him, saw that he had faith to be healed and called out, "Stand up on your feet!" At that, the man jumped up and began to walk.

Acts 14:8-10 NIV

And God did unusual and extraordinary miracles by the hands of Paul,

so that handkerchiefs or towels or aprons which had touched his skin were carried away and put upon the sick, and their diseases left them and the evil spirits came out of them.

Acts 19:11-12 AMP

And it came to pass, that the father of Publius lay sick of a fever and of a bloody flux: to whom Paul entered in, and prayed, and laid his hands on him, and healed him.

So when this was done, others also, which had diseases in the island, came, and were healed:

Acts 28:8-9

As it is written: "I have made you a father of many nations." He is our father in the sight of God, in whom he believed—the God who gives life to the dead and calls into being things that were not.

Against all hope, Abraham in hope believed and so became the father of many nations, just as it had been said to him, "So shall your offspring be."

Without weakening in his faith, he faced the fact that his body was as good as dead—since he was about a hundred years old—and that Sarah's womb was also dead.

Yet he did not waver through unbelief regarding the promise of God, but was strengthened in his faith and gave glory to God, being fully persuaded that God had power to do what he had promised.

Romans 4:17-21 NIV

But if the Spirit of him that raised up Jesus from the dead dwell in you, he that raised up Christ from the dead shall also quicken your mortal bodies by his Spirit that dwelleth in you.

Therefore, brethren, we are debtors, not to the flesh, to live after the flesh.

For if ye live after the flesh, ye shall die: but if ye through the Spirit do mortify the deeds of the body, ye shall live.

Romans 8:11-13

For the creation was subjected to frustration, not by its own choice, but by the will of the one who subjected it, in hope

And he who searches our hearts knows the mind of the Spirit, because the Spirit intercedes for God's people in accordance with the will of God.

Romans 8:20,27 NIV

Now about the gifts of the Spirit, brothers and sisters, I do not want you to be uninformed.

You know that when you were pagans, somehow or other you were influenced and led astray to mute idols.

Therefore I want you to know that no one who is speaking by the Spirit of God says, "Jesus be cursed," and no one can say, "Jesus is Lord," except by the Holy Spirit.

There are different kinds of gifts, but the same Spirit distributes them.

There are different kinds of service, but the same Lord.

There are different kinds of working, but in all of them and in everyone it is the same God at work.

Now to each one the manifestation of the Spirit is given for the common good.

To one there is given through the Spirit a message of wisdom, to another a message of knowledge by means of the same Spirit, to another faith by the same Spirit, to another gifts of healing by that one Spirit,

to another miraculous powers, to another prophecy, to another distinguishing between spirits, to another speaking in different kinds of tongues, and to still another the interpretation of tongues.

All these are the work of one and the same Spirit, and he distributes them to each one, just as he determines.

I Corinthians 12:1-11 NIV

And God has appointed these in the church: first apostles, second prophets, third teachers, after that miracles, then gifts of healings, helps, administrations, varieties of tongues.

Are all apostles? Are all prophets? Are all teachers? Are all workers of miracles?

Do all have gifts of healings? Do all speak with tongues? Do all interpret?

But earnestly desire the best gifts. And yet show you a more excellent way.

1 Corinthians 12:28-31 NKJV

We are human, but we don't wage war as humans do.

We use God's mighty weapons, not worldly weapons, to

knock down the strongholds of human reasoning and to destroy false arguments. We destroy every proud obstacle that keeps people from knowing God. We capture their rebellious thoughts and teach them to obey Christ.

2 Corinthians 10:3-5 NLT

For though we live in the world, we do not wage war as the world does. The weapons we fight with are not the weapons of the world. On the contrary, they have divine power to demolish strongholds.

We demolish arguments and every pretension that sets itself up against the knowledge of God, and we take captive every thought to make it obedient to Christ.

2 Corinthians 10:3-5 NIV

Christ hath redeemed us from the curse of the law, being made a curse for us: for it is written, Cursed is every one that hangeth on a tree:

That the blessing of Abraham might come on the Gentiles through Jesus Christ; that we might receive the promise of the Spirit through faith.

And if ye be Christ's, then are ye Abraham's seed, and heirs according to the promise

Galatians 3: 13-14, 29

Children, obey your parents because you belong to the Lord, for this is the right thing to do.

"Honor your father and mother." This is the first commandment with a promise:

If you honor your father and mother, "things will go well for you, and you will have a long life on the earth."

Ephesians 6:1-3 NLT

In conclusion, be strong in the Lord [be empowered through your union with Him]; draw your strength from Him [that strength which His boundless might provides].

Put on God's whole armor [the armor of a heavy-armed soldier which God supplies], that you may be able successfully to stand up against [all] the strategies and the deceits of the devil.

For we are not wrestling with flesh and blood [contending only with physical opponents], but against the despotisms, against the powers, against [the master spirits who are] the world rulers of this present darkness, against the spirit forces of wickedness in the heavenly (supernatural) sphere.

Therefore put on God's complete armor, that you may be able to resist and stand your ground on the evil day [of danger], and, having done all [the crisis demands], to stand [firmly in your place].

Stand therefore [hold your ground], having tightened the belt of truth around your loins and having put on the breastplate of integrity and of moral rectitude and right standing with God,

and having shod your feet in preparation [to face the enemy with the firm-footed stability, the promptness, and the readiness produced by the good news] of the Gospel of peace.

Lift up over all the [covering] shield of saving faith, upon which you can quench all the flaming missiles of the wicked [one].

And take the helmet of salvation and the sword that the Spirit wields, which is the Word of God.

Pray at all times (on every occasion, in every season) in the Spirit, with all [manner of] prayer and entreaty.

To that end keep alert and watch with strong purpose and perseverance, interceding in behalf of all the saints (God's consecrated people).

Ephesians 6:10-18 AMP

Being confident of this very thing, that He who has begun a good work in you will complete it until the day of Jesus Christ;

Philippians 1:6 NKJV

Let this mind be in you which was also in Christ Jesus,

who, being in the form of God, did not consider it robbery to be equal with God,

but made Himself of no reputation, taking the form of a bondservant, and coming in the likeness of men.

And being found in appearance as a man, He humbled Himself and became obedient to the point of death, even the death of the cross.

Therefore God also has highly exalted Him and given Him the name which is above every name,

that at the name of Jesus every knee should bow, of those in heaven, and of those on earth, and of those under the earth,

and that every tongue should confess that Jesus Christ is Lord, to the glory of God the Father.

Philippians 2:5-11 NKJV

And the very God of peace sanctify you wholly; and I pray God your whole spirit and soul and body be preserved blameless unto the coming of our Lord Jesus Christ.

1 Thessalonians 5:23

But women will be saved through child-   bearing if they continue in faith, love and holiness with propriety.

1 Timothy 2;15 NIV

Since we have a great high priest, Jesus the Son of God, who has gone into heaven, let us hold on to the faith we have.

For our high priest is able to understand our weaknesses. He was tempted in every way that we are, but he did not sin.

Let us, then, feel very sure that we can come before God's throne where there is grace. There we can receive mercy and grace to help us when we need it.

Hebrews 4:14-16 NCV

Then you will not become spiritually dull and indifferent. Instead, you will follow the example of those who are going to inherit God's promises because of their faith and endurance.

For example, there was God's promise to Abraham. Since there was no one greater to

swear by, God took an oath in his own name, saying:

"I will certainly bless you, and I will multiply your descen-dants beyond number."

Hebrews 6:12-14 NLT

Let us hold fast the profession of our faith without wavering; (for he is faithful that promised;)...

Hebrews 10:23

Therefore do not cast away your confidence, which has great reward.

For you have need of endurance, so that after you have done the will of God, you may receive the promise:

Hebrews 10:35-36 NKJV

But without faith it is impossible to please him: for he that cometh to God must believe that he is, and that he is a rewarder of them that diligently seek him.

Hebrews 11:6

Look after each other so that none of you fails to receive the grace of God. Watch out that no poisonous root of bitterness grows up to trouble you, corrupting many.

Hebrews 12:15 NLT

Jesus Christ is the same yesterday, today, and forever.

Hebrews 13:8 NKJV

Is anyone among you in trouble? Let them pray. Is anyone happy? Let them sing songs of praise.

Is anyone among you sick? Let them call the elders of the church to pray over them and anoint them with oil in the name of the Lord.

And the prayer offered in faith will make the sick person well; the Lord will raise them up.

If they have sinned, they will be forgiven.

Therefore confess your sins to each other and pray for each other so that you may be healed. The prayer of a righteous person is powerful and effective.

James 5:13-16 NIV

He personally carried the load of our sins in his own body when he died on the cross, so that we can be finished with sin and live a good life from now on. For his wounds have healed ours!

1 Peter 2:24 TLB

He Himself bore our sins in His body on the cross, so that we might die to sin and live to righteousness; for by His wounds you were healed.

1 Peter 2:24 NASB

In the same way, you who are younger, submit yourselves to your elders. All of you, clothe yourselves with humility toward one another, because, "God opposes the proud but shows favor to the humble."

Humble yourselves, therefore, under God's mighty hand, that he may lift you up in due time.

Cast all your anxiety on him because he cares for you.

Be alert and of sober mind. Your enemy the devil prowls around like a roaring lion looking for someone to devour.

Resist him, standing firm in the faith, because you know that the family of believers throughout the world is undergoing the same kind of sufferings.

And the God of all grace, who called you to his eternal glory in Christ, after you have suffered a little while, will himself restore you and make you strong, firm and steadfast.

1 Peter 5:5-10 NIV

You, dear children, are from God and have overcome them,
because the one who is in you is greater than the one who is in the world.

1 John 4:4 NIV

And we are confident that he hears us whenever we ask for anything that pleases him.

And since we know he hears us when we make our requests, we also know that he will give us what we ask for.

1 John 5:14-15 NLT

Beloved, I wish above all things that thou mayest prosper and be in health, even as thy soul prospereth.

3 John 2:1 KJV

My heartfelt prayer for you, my very dear friend, is that you may be as healthy and prosperous in every way are you are in soul.

3 John 2:1 Phillips

And they overcame him by the blood of the Lamb, and by the word of their testimony.

Revelation 12:11

Finances Scriptures
Old Testament

While the earth remains, seedtime and harvest, cold and heat, winter and summer, and day and night shall not cease.

Genesis 8:22 NKJV

And God blessed Noah and his sons, and said unto them, Be fruitful, and multiply, and replenish the earth.

Genesis 9:1

I will make you into a great nation, and I will bless you; I will make your name great, and you will be a blessing.
I will bless those who bless you, and whoever curses you I will curse; and all peoples on earth will be blessed through you.

Genesis 12:2-3 NIV

Then Melchizedek king of Salem brought out bread and wine. He was priest of God Most High, and he blessed Abram,

saying,

"Blessed be Abram by God Most High, Creator of heaven and earth. And praise be to God Most High, who delivered your enemies into your hand."

Then Abram gave him a tenth of everything.

The king of Sodom said to Abram, "Give me the people and keep the goods for yourself."

But Abram said to the king of Sodom, "With raised hand I have sworn an oath to the Lord,

God Most High, Creator of heaven and earth,
that I will accept nothing belonging to you, not even a thread or the strap of a sandal, so that you will never be able to say, 'I made Abram rich.' I will accept nothing but what my men have eaten and the share that belongs to the men who went with me—to Aner, Eshkol and Mamre. Let them have their share."

Genesis 14:18-24 NIV

When Abram was ninety-nine years old, the Lord appeared to him and said, "I am God Almighty. Obey me and do what is right. I will make an agreement between us, and I will make you the ancestor of many people."

Then Abram bowed facedown on the ground. God said" I am making my agreement

with you: I will make you the father of many
nations. I am changing your name from Abram to Abraham
because I am making you a father of many nations. I will give
you many descendants. New nations will be born from you,
and kings will come from you. And I will make an agreement
between me and you and all your descendants from now on: I
will be your God and the God of all your descendants."

Genesis 17:1-7 NCV

And God said unto Abraham, As for Sarai thy wife, thou
shalt not call her name Sarai, but Sarah shall her name be.

And I will bless her, and give thee a son also of her: yea, I will
bless her, and she shall be a mother of nations; kings of people
shall be of her.

Genesis 17:15-16

And the Lord said, Shall I hide from Abraham that thing
which I do; Seeing that Abraham shall surely become a great
and mighty nation, and all the nations of the earth shall be
blessed in him?

For I know him, that he will command his children and his
household after him, and they shall keep the way of the Lord, to

do justice and judgment; that the Lord may bring upon Abraham that which he hath spoken of him.

Genesis 18:17-19

Then the angel of the Lord called to Abraham a second time from heaven, and said, "By Myself I have sworn, declares the LORD, because you have done this thing and have not withheld your son, your only son, indeed I will greatly bless you, and I will greatly multiply your seed as the stars of the heavens and as the sand which is on the seashore; and your seed shall possess the gate of their enemies. In your seed all the nations of the earth shall be blessed, because you have obeyed My voice."

Genesis 22:15-18 NASB

Abraham was now very old, and the Lord had blessed him in every way.

Genesis 24:1 NIV

Now there was a famine in the land—besides the previous famine in Abraham's time—and Isaac went to Abimelek king of the Philistines in Gerar.

The Lord appeared to Isaac and said, "Do not go down to

Egypt; live in the land where I tell you to live. Stay in this land for a while, and I will be with you and will bless you. For to you and your descendants I will give all these lands and will confirm the oath I swore to your father Abraham.

"I will make your descendants as numerous as the stars in the sky and will give them all these lands, and through your offspring all nations on earth will be blessed, because Abraham obeyed me and did everything I required of him, keeping my commands, my decrees and my instructions."

Genesis 26:1-5 NIV

Then Isaac sowed in that land, and reaped in the same year a hundredfold; and the Lord blessed him. The man began to prosper, and continued prospering until he became very prosperous; for he had possessions of flocks and possessions of herds and a great number of servants.
So the Philistines envied him.

Genesis 26:12-14 NKJV

The Lord appeared to him on the night of his arrival. "I am the God of your father, Abraham," he said. "Do not be afraid, for I am with you and will bless you. I will multiply your descendants, and they will become a great nation. I will do this because of my promise to Abraham, my servant."

Genesis 26:24 NLT

May God Almighty bless you and give you many children. And may your descendants multiply and become many nations!

Genesis 28:3 NLT

Thus the man became exceedingly prosperous, and had large flocks, female and male servants, and camels and donkeys.

Genesis 30:43 NKJV

Joseph is a fruitful vine, a fruitful vine near a spring, whose branches climb over a wall. With bitterness archers attacked him; they shot at him with hostility.

But his bow remained steady, his strong arms stayed limber, because of the hand of the Mighty One of Jacob, because of the Shepherd, the Rock of Israel, because of your father's God, who helps you, because of the Almighty, who blesses you with blessings of the skies above, blessings of the deep springs below, blessings of the breast and womb.

Your father's blessings are greater than the blessings of the ancient mountains, than the bounty of the age-old hills. Let all these rest on the head of Joseph, on the brow of the prince among his brothers.

Genesis 49:22-26 NIV

And the Lord said, I have surely seen the affliction of my people which are in Egypt, and have heard their cry by reason of their taskmasters; for I know their sorrows;

And I am come down to deliver them out of the hand of the Egyptians, and to bring them up out of that land unto a good land and a large, unto a land flowing with milk and honey.

Exodus 3:7-8

And ye shall serve the Lord your God, and he shall bless thy bread, and thy water

Exodus 23:25a

"And Bezalel and Aholiab, and every gifted artisan in whom the Lord has put wisdom and understanding, to know how to do all manner of work for the service of the sanctuary, shall do according to all that the Lord has commanded."

Then Moses called Bezalel and Aholiab, and every gifted artisan in whose heart the Lord had put wisdom, everyone whose heart was stirred, to come and do the work. And they received from Moses all the offering which the children of Israel had brought for the work of the service of making the sanctuary. So they continued bringing to him free will offerings every morning. Then all the craftsmen who were doing all the work of the sanctuary came, each from the work he was doing, and they spoke to Moses, saying, "The people bring much more than enough for the service of the work which the Lord commanded us to do."

So Moses gave a commandment, and they caused it to be proclaimed throughout the camp, saying, "Let neither man nor woman do any more work for the offering of the sanctuary." And the people were restrained from bringing, for the material they had was sufficient for all the work to be done—indeed too much.

Exodus 36:1-7 NKJV

If you walk in My statutes and keep My commandments so as to carry them out, then I shall give you rains in their season, so that the land will yield its produce and the trees of the field will bear their fruit.

Indeed, your threshing will last for you until grape gathering, and grape gathering will last until sowing time. You will thus eat your food to the full and live securely in your land. I shall also grant peace in the land, so that you may lie down with no one making you tremble. I shall also eliminate harmful beasts from the land, and no sword will pass through your land.

But you will chase your enemies and they will fall before you by the sword; five of you will chase a hundred, and a hundred of you will chase ten thousand, and your enemies will fall before you by the sword.

So I will turn toward you and make you fruitful and multiply you, and I will confirm My covenant with you.

You will eat the old supply and clear out the old because of the new.

Moreover, I will make My dwelling among you, and My soul will not reject you. I will also walk among you and be your God, and you shall be My people. I am the Lord your God, who brought you out of the land of Egypt so that you would not be their slaves, and I broke the bars of your yoke and made you walk erect.

Leviticus 26:3-13 NASB

A tithe of everything from the land, whether grain from the soil or fruit from the trees, belongs to the Lord; it is holy to the Lord.

Whoever would redeem any of their tithe must add a fifth of the value to it.

Every tithe of the herd and flock—every tenth animal that passes under the shepherd's rod—will be holy to the Lord.

No one may pick out the good from the bad or make any substitution. If anyone does make a substitution, both the animal and its substitute become holy and cannot be redeemed.

These are the commands the Lord gave Moses at Mount Sinai for the Israelites.

Leviticus 27:30-34 NIV

'May the Lord bless you and protect you. May the Lord smile on you and be gracious to you. May the Lord show you his favor and give you his peace.'

Whenever Aaron and his sons bless the people of Israel in my name, I myself will bless them.

Numbers 6:24-27 NLT

If the Lord is pleased with us, he will lead us into that land and give us that fertile land.

Numbers 14:8 NCV

God is not a man, that he should lie; neither the son of man, that he should repent: hath he said, and shall he not do it? or hath he spoken, and shall he not make it good?

Behold, I have received commandment to bless: and he hath blessed; and I cannot reverse it.

Numbers 23: 19-20

See, I have given you this land, so go in and take it for yourselves. The Lord promised it to your ancestors—Abraham, Isaac, and Jacob and their descendants.

At that time I said, "I am not able to take care of you by myself. The LORD your God has made you grow in number so that there are as many of you as there are stars in the sky. I pray that the LORD, the God of your ancestors, will give you a thousand times more people and do all the wonderful things he promised.

Deuteronomy 1:8-11 NCV

For the Lord your God has blessed you in all the work of your hand. He knows your walking through this great wilderness. These forty years the Lord your God has been with you; you have lacked nothing.

Deuteronomy 2:7 AMP

Therefore know that the Lord your God, He is God, the faithful God who keeps covenant and mercy for a thousand generations with those who love Him and keep His commandments;

Deuteronomy 7:9 NKJV

Then it shall come to pass, because you listen to these judgments, and keep and do them, that the LORD your God will keep with you the covenant and the mercy which He swore to your fathers.

And He will love you and bless you and multiply you; He will also bless the fruit of your womb and the fruit of your land, your grain and your new wine and your oil, the increase of your cattle and the offspring of your flock, in the land of which He swore to your fathers to give you.

You shall be blessed above all peoples; there shall not be a male or female barren among you or among your livestock.

Deuteronomy 7:12-14 NKJV

Observe the commands of the Lord your God, walking in obedience to him and revering him. For the Lord your God is bringing you into a good land—a land with brooks, streams, and deep springs gushing out into the valleys and hills; a land with wheat and barley, vines and fig trees, pomegranates, olive oil and honey; a land where bread will not be scarce and you will lack nothing; a land where the rocks are iron and you can dig copper out of the hills.

When you have eaten and are satisfied, praise the Lord your God for the good land he has given you. Be careful that you do not forget the Lord your God, failing to observe his commands, his laws and his decrees that I am giving you this day. Otherwise, when you eat and are satisfied, when you build fine houses and settle down, and when your herds and flocks grow large and your silver and gold increase and all you have is multiplied, then your heart will become proud and you will forget the Lord your God, who brought you out of Egypt, out of the land of slavery. He led you through the vast and dreadful wilderness, that thirsty and waterless land, with its venomous snakes and scorpions. He brought you water out of hard rock. He gave you manna to eat in the wilderness, something your ancestors had never known, to humble and test you so that in the end it might go well with you. You may say to yourself, "My power and the strength of my hands have produced this wealth for me." But remember the LORD your God, for it is he who gives you the ability to produce wealth, and so confirms his covenant, which he swore to your ancestors, as it is today.

Deuteronomy 8:6-18 NIV

So obey all the commands I am giving you today so that you will be strong and can go in and take the land you are going to take as your own.

Then you will live a long time in the land that the Lord promised to give to your ancestors and their descendants, a fertile land.

Deuteronomy 11:8-9 NCV

There, in the presence of the Lord your God, you and your families shall eat and shall rejoice in everything you have put your hand to, because the Lord your God has blessed you.

Deuteronomy 12:7 NIV

You shall surely tithe all the produce from what you sow, which comes out of the field every year.

Deuteronomy 14:22 NASB

For the Lord thy God blesseth thee, as he promised thee: and thou shalt lend unto many nations, but thou shalt not borrow; and thou shalt reign over many nations, but they shall not reign over thee.

If there be among you a poor man of one of thy brethren within any of thy gates in thy land which the LORD thy God giveth thee, thou shalt not harden thine heart, nor shut thine hand from thy poor brother:

But thou shalt open thine hand wide unto him, and shalt surely lend him sufficient for his need, in that which he wanteth.

Thou shalt surely give him, and thine heart shall not be grieved when thou givest unto him: because that for this thing the LORD thy God shall bless thee in all thy works, and in all that thou puttest thine hand unto.

For the poor shall never cease out of the land: therefore I command thee, saying, Thou shalt open thine hand wide unto thy brother, to thy poor, and to thy needy, in thy land.

Deuteronomy 15:6-8, 10, 11

Every man shall give as he is able, according to the blessing of the Lord thy God which he hath given thee.

Deuteronomy 16:17

When you make a vow to the Lord your God, you shall not delay to pay it, for it would be sin in you, and the Lord your God will surely require it of you.

However, if you refrain from vowing, it would not be sin in you.

You shall be careful to perform what goes out from your lips, just as you have voluntarily vowed to the Lord your God, what you have promised.

Deuteronomy 23:21-23 NASB

If you fully obey the Lord your God and carefully follow all his commands I give you today, the Lord your God will set you high above all the nations on earth. All these blessings will come on you and accompany you if you obey the Lord your God: You will be blessed in the city and blessed in the country. The fruit of your womb will be blessed, and the crops of your land and the young of your livestock—the calves of your herds and the lambs of your flocks.

Your basket and your kneading trough will be blessed. You will be blessed when you come in and blessed when you go out.

The Lord will grant that the enemies who rise up against you will be defeated before you. They will come at you from one direction but flee from you in seven.

The Lord will send a blessing on your barns and on everything you put your hand to. The Lord your God will bless you in the land he is giving you.

The Lord will establish you as his holy people, as he promised you on oath, if you keep the commands of the Lord your God and walk in obedience to him. Then all the peoples on earth will see that you are called by the name of the Lord, and they will fear you. The Lord will grant you abundant prosperity—in the fruit of your womb, the young of your livestock and the crops of your ground—in the land he swore to your ancestors to give you.

The Lord will open the heavens, the storehouse of his bounty, to send rain on your land in season and to bless all the work of your hands. You will lend to many nations but will borrow from none. The Lord will make you the head, not the tail. If you pay attention to the commands of the Lord your God that I give you this day and carefully follow them, you will always be at the top, never at the bottom. Do not turn aside from any of the commands I give you today, to the right or to the left, following other gods and serving them.

Deuteronomy 28:1-14 NIV

Therefore, obey the terms of this covenant so that you will prosper in everything you do.

Deuteronomy 29:9 NLT

Then the Lord your God will make you most prosperous in all the work of your hands and in the fruit of your womb, the young of your livestock and the crops of your land. The Lord will again delight in you and make you prosperous, just as he delighted in your ancestors, if you obey the Lord your God and keep his commands and decrees that are written in this Book of the Law and turn to the Lord your God with all your heart and with all your soul.

Deuteronomy 30:9-10 NIV

Look at what I've done for you today: I've placed in front of you Life and Good, Death and Evil. And I command you today: Love God, your God. Walk in his ways. Keep his commandments, regulations, and rules so that you will live, really live, live exuberantly, blessed by God, your God, in the land you are about to enter and possess.

Deuteronomy 30:15-16 MSG

I call heaven and earth to record this day against you, that I have set before you life and death, blessing and cursing: therefore choose life, that both thou and thy seed may live:

That thou mayest love the Lord thy God, and that thou mayest obey his voice, and that thou mayest cleave unto him: for he is thy life, and the length of thy days: that thou mayest dwell in the land which the Lord sware unto thy fathers, to Abraham, to Isaac, and to Jacob, to give them.

Deuteronomy 30:19-20

I will give you every place where you set your foot, as I promised Moses.

Joshua 1:3 NIV

Only be strong and very courageous, that you may observe to do according to all the law which Moses My servant commanded you; do not turn from it to the right hand or to the left, that you may prosper wherever you go. This Book of the Law shall not depart from your mouth, but you shall meditate in it day and night, that you may observe to do according to all that is written in it. For then you will make your way prosperous, and then you will have good success.

Joshua 1:7-8 NKJV

The wife of a man from the company of the prophets cried out to Elisha, "Your servant my husband is dead, and you know that he revered the Lord. But now his creditor is coming to take my two boys as his slaves."

Elisha replied to her, "How can I help you? Tell me, what do you have in your house?"

"Your servant has nothing there at all," she said, "except a small jar of olive oil."

Elisha said, "Go around and ask all your neighbors for empty jars. Don't ask for just a few. Then go inside and shut the door behind you and your sons. Pour oil into all the jars, and as each is filled, put it to one side."

She left him and shut the door behind her and her sons. They brought the jars to her and she kept pouring. When all the jars were full, she said to her son, "Bring me another one."

But he replied, "There is not a jar left." Then the oil stopped flowing.

She went and told the man of God, and he said, "Go, sell the oil and pay your debts.

You and your sons can live on what is left."

2 Kings 4:1-7 NIV

For you are God, O Lord. And you have promised these good things to your servant. And now, it has pleased you to bless the house of your servant, so that it will continue forever before you. For when you grant a blessing, O Lord, it is an eternal blessing!

1 Chronicles 17:26-27 NLT

Only the Lord give thee wisdom and understanding, and give thee charge concerning Israel, that thou mayest keep the law of the Lord thy God. Then shalt thou prosper, if thou takest heed to fulfil the statutes and judgments which the LORD charged Moses with concerning Israel: be strong, and of good courage; dread not, nor be dismayed.

1 Chronicles 22:12-13

Riches and honor come from you. You rule everything. You have the power and strength to make anyone great and strong.

1 Chronicles 29:12 NCV

And he died in a good old age, full of days, riches, and honour.

1 Chronicles 29:28

Jehoshaphat had riches and honor in abundance.

2 Chronicles18:1 NKJV

Believe in the Lord your God, so shall ye be established; believe his prophets, so shall ye prosper.

2 Chronicles 20:20

And he did that which was right in the sight of the Lord, according to all that his father Amaziah did.

And he sought God in the days of Zechariah, who had understanding in the visions of God: and as long as he sought the Lord, God made him to prosper.

2 Chronicles 26:4-5

He ordered the people living in Jerusalem to give the portion due the priests and Levites so they could devote themselves to the Law of the Lord.

As soon as the order went out, the Israelites generously gave the firstfruits of their grain, new wine, olive oil and honey and all that the fields produced. They brought a great amount, a tithe of everything.

The people of Israel and Judah who lived in the towns of Judah also brought a tithe of their herds and flocks and a tithe of the holy things dedicated to the Lord their God, and they piled them in heaps.

They began doing this in the third month and finished in the seventh month.When Hezekiah and his officials came and saw the heaps, they praised the LORD and blessed his people Israel.

Hezekiah asked the priests and Levites about the heaps; and Azariah the chief priest, from the family of Zadok, answered, "Since the people began to bring their contributions to the temple of the Lord, we have had enough to eat and plenty to spare, because the Lord has blessed his people, and this great amount is left over."

Hezekiah gave orders to prepare storerooms in the temple of the Lord, and this was done.

Then they faithfully brought in the contributions, tithes and dedicated gifts.

2 Chronicles 31:4-12 NIV

Thus Hezekiah did throughout all Judah, and he did what was good and right and true before the Lord his God. And in every work that he began in the service of the house of God, in the law and in the commandment, to seek his God, he did it with all his heart. So he prospered.

2 Chronicles 31:20-21 NKJV

I answered them, The God of heaven will prosper us; therefore we His servants will arise and build.

Nehemiah 2:20 AMP

"Indeed, forty years You provided for them in the wilderness and they were not in want; Their clothes did not wear out, nor did their feet swell.

"You also gave them kingdoms and peoples, And allotted them to them as a boundary. They took possession of the land of Sihon the king of Heshbon And the land of Og the king of Bashan.

"You made their sons numerous as the stars of heaven, And You brought them into the land which You had told their fathers to enter and possess.

"So their sons entered and possessed the land. And You subdued before them the inhabitants of the land, the Canaanites, And You gave them into their hand, with their kings and the peoples of the land, To do with them as they desired.

"They captured fortified cities and a fertile land. They took possession of houses full of every good thing, Hewn cisterns, vineyards, olive groves, Fruit trees in abundance. So they ate, were filled and grew fat, And reveled in Your great goodness."

Nehemiah 9:21-25 NASB

Your beginnings will seem humble, so prosperous will your future be.

Job 8:7 NIV

If they obey and serve him, they shall spend their days in prosperity, and their years in pleasures.

Job 36:11

The Lord blessed the latter part of Job's life more than the former part. He had fourteen thousand sheep, six thousand camels, a thousand yoke of oxen and a thousand donkeys. And he also had seven sons and three daughters.

After this, Job lived a hundred and forty years; he saw his children and their children to the fourth generation.

And so Job died, an old man and full of years.

Job 42: 12-13, 16, 17 NIV

Blessed is the man who walks not in the counsel of the ungodly, nor stands in the path of sinners, nor sits in the seat of the scornful;

But his delight is in the law of the LORD, and in His law he meditates day and night. He shall be like a tree planted by the rivers of water, that brings forth its fruit in its season, whose leaf also shall not wither; and whatever he does shall prosper.

Psalm 1:1-3 NKJV

May your blessing be on your people.

Psalm 3:8 NIV

For You, Lord, will bless the [uncompromisingly] righteous [him who is upright and in right standing with You]; as with a shield You will surround him with goodwill (pleasure and favor).

Psalm 5:12 AMP

The law of the Lord is perfect, restoring the [whole] person; the testimony of the Lord is sure, making wise the simple.

The precepts of the Lord are right, rejoicing the heart; the commandment of the Lord is pure and bright, enlightening the eyes.

The [reverent] fear of the Lord is clean, enduring forever; the ordinances of the Lord are true and righteous altogether.

More to be desired are they than gold, even than much fine gold; they are sweeter also than honey and drippings from the honeycomb.

Moreover, by them is Your servant warned (reminded, illuminated, and instructed); and in keeping them there is great reward.

Psalm 19:7-11 AMP

The Lord is my shepherd; I have all that I need.

He lets me rest in green meadows; he leads me beside peaceful streams. He renews my strength. He guides me along right paths, bringing honor to his name.

Even when I walk through the darkest valley, I will not be afraid, for you are close beside me. Your rod and your staff protect and comfort me.

You prepare a feast for me in the presence of my enemies. You honor me by anointing my head with oil. My cup overflows with blessings.

Surely your goodness and unfailing love will pursue me all the days of my life, and I will live in the house of the Lord forever.

Psalm 23:1-6 NLT

Blessed is the nation whose God is the Lord; and the people whom he hath chosen for his own inheritance.

Psalm 33:12

The lions may grow weak and hungry, but those who seek the Lord lack no good thing.

Psalm 34:10 NIV

Even strong young lions sometimes go hungry, but those who trust in the Lord will lack no good thing.

Psalm 34:10 NLT

Let them shout for joy and rejoice, who favor my vindication; And let them say continually, "The Lord be magnified, Who delights in the prosperity of His servant."

Psalm 35:27 NASB

Day by day the Lord takes care of the innocent, and they will receive an inheritance that lasts forever.

They will not be disgraced in hard times; even in famine they will have more than enough.

Psalm 37: 18-19 NLT

For such as be blessed of him shall inherit the earth.

Psalm 37:22

I have been young and now I am old. And in all my years I have never seen the Lord forsake a man who loves him; nor have I seen the children of the godly go hungry.

Instead, the godly are able to be generous with their gifts and loans to others, and their children are a blessing.

Psalm 37:25-26 TLB

For every beast of the forest is Mine, and the cattle upon a thousand hills or upon the mountains where thousands are.

Psalm 50:10 AMP

If riches increase, Do not set your heart on them.

Psalm 62:10 NKJV

You let people ride over our heads; we went through fire and water, but you brought us to a place of abundance.

Psalm 66:12 NIV

The land yields its harvest; God, our God, blesses us.

May God bless us still, so that all the ends of the earth will fear him.

Psalm 67:6-7 NIV

For the Lord God is a sun and shield: the Lord will give grace and glory: no good thing will he withhold from them that walk uprightly.

Psalm 84:11

For Jehovah God is our Light and our Protector. He gives us grace and glory. No good thing will he withhold from those who walk along his paths.

O Lord of the armies of heaven, blessed are those who trust in you.

Psalm 84:11-12 TLB

Give to the Lord, O families of the peoples, Give to the Lord glory and strength.

Give to the Lord the glory due His name; Bring an offering, and come into His courts.

Psalm 96:7-8 NKJV

Give to the Lord, O families of the peoples, Give to the Lord glory and strength. Give to the Lord the glory due His name; Bring an offering, and come into His courts.

Psalm 104:24 NIV

And the Lord multiplied the people of Israel until they became too mighty for their enemies.

Psalm 105:24 NLT

Then he brought his people out, and they carried with them silver and gold. Not one of his people stumbled.

Psalm 105:37 NCV

Praise the Lord! Blessed is the man who fears the Lord, who delights greatly in His commandments.

His descendants will be mighty on earth; the generation of the upright will be blessed.

Wealth and riches will be in his house, and his righteousness endures forever.

Unto the upright there arises light in the darkness; He is gracious, and full of compassion, and righteous.

A good man deals graciously and lends; He will guide his affairs with discretion.

Psalm 112:1-5 NKJV

The Lord remembers us and will bless us: He will bless his people Israel, he will bless the house of Aaron, he will bless those who fear the Lord—small and great alike.

May the Lord cause you to flourish, both you and your children.

May you be blessed by the Lord, the Maker of heaven and earth.

Psalm 115:12-15 NIV

Joyful are people of integrity, who follow the instructions of the Lord.

Joyful are those who obey his laws and search for him with all their hearts.

Psalm 119:1-2 NLT

Pray for the peace of Jerusalem: they shall prosper that love thee.

Peace be within thy walls, and prosperity within thy palaces.

Psalm 122:6-7

Blessed is every one who fears the Lord, who walks in His ways.

When you eat the labor of your hands, you shall be happy,

and it shall be well with you.

Your wife shall be like a fruitful vine in the very heart of your house, your children like olive plants all around your table.

Behold, thus shall the man be blessed who fears the Lord.

The Lord bless you out of Zion, And may you see the good of Jerusalem all the days of your life.

Yes, may you see your children's children. Peace be upon Israel!

Psalm 128:1-6 NKJV

I will bless her with abundant provisions; her poor I will satisfy with food.

Psalm 132:15 NIV

Honor the Lord with your wealth, with the firstfruits of all your crops; then your barns will be filled to overflowing, and your vats will brim over with new wine

Proverbs 3:9-10 NIV

Happy is the man who finds wisdom, and the man who gains understanding;

For her proceeds are better than the profits of silver, and her gain than fine gold.

She is more precious than rubies, and all the things you may desire cannot compare with her.

Length of days is in her right hand, in her left hand riches and honor.

Proverbs 3:13-16 NKJV

Do not withhold good from those who deserve it when it's in your power to help them.

If you can help your neighbor now, don't say, "Come back tomorrow, and then I'll help you."

Don't plot harm against your neighbor, for those who live nearby trust you.

The Lord curses the house of the wicked, but he blesses the home of the upright.

Proverbs 3:27-29, 33 NLT

You sleep a little; you take a nap. You fold your hands and lie down to rest.

So you will be as poor as if you had been robbed; you will have as little as if you had been held up.

Proverbs 6:10-11 NCV

Men do not despise a thief, if he steal to satisfy his soul when he is hungry;

But if he be found, he shall restore sevenfold; he shall give all the substance of his house.

Proverbs 6:30-31

Riches and honor are with me, enduring wealth and righteousness (uprightness in every area and relation, and right standing with God).

My fruit is better than gold, yes, than refined gold, and my increase than choice silver.

I [Wisdom] walk in the way of righteousness (moral and spiritual rectitude in every area and relation), in the midst of the paths of justice, that I may cause those who love me to inherit [true] riches and that I may fill their treasuries.

Proverbs 8:18-21 AMP

Now therefore listen to me, O you sons; for blessed (happy, fortunate, to be envied) are those who keep my ways.

Hear instruction and be wise, and do not refuse or neglect it.

Blessed (happy, fortunate, to be envied) is the man who listens to me, watching daily at my gates, waiting at the posts of my doors.

For whoever finds me [Wisdom] finds life and draws forth and obtains favor from the Lord.

Proverbs 8:32-35 AMP

The Lord does not let the righteous go hungry, but he thwarts the craving of the wicked.

Lazy hands make for poverty, but diligent hands bring wealth.

Proverbs 10:3-4 NIV

It is the blessing of the Lord that makes rich, and He adds no sorrow to it.

Proverbs 10:22 NASB

The desire of the righteous shall be granted.

Proverbs 10:24

There is one who scatters, and yet increases all the more, and there is one who withholds what is justly due, and yet it results only in want.

The generous man will be prosperous, and he who waters will

himself be watered.

He who withholds grain, the people will curse him, but blessing will be on the head of him who sells it.

He who diligently seeks good seeks favor, But he who seeks evil, evil will come to him.

He who trusts in his riches will fall, but the righteous will flourish like the green leaf.

Proverbs 11:24-28 NASB

The soul of the sluggard desireth, and hath nothing: but the soul of the diligent shall be made fat.

Wealth gotten by vanity shall be diminished: but he that gathereth by labour shall increase.

Proverbs 13:4,11

Poverty and shame will come to him who disdains correction, but he who regards a rebuke will be honored.

Proverbs 13:18 NKJV

A good man leaveth an inheritance to his children's children: and the wealth of the sinner is laid up for the just.

Proverbs 13:22

The godly eat to their hearts' content, but the belly of the wicked goes hungry.

Proverbs 13:25 NLT

It is a sin to hate your neighbor, but being kind to the needy brings happiness

Proverbs 14:21 NCV

All hard work brings a profit, but mere talk leads only to poverty.

Proverbs 14:23 NIV

In the house of the righteous is much treasure: but in the revenues of the wicked is trouble.

Proverbs 15:6

The Lord will destroy the house of the proud: but he will establish the border of the widow.

Proverbs 15:25

But he who hates bribes will live.

Proverbs 15:27 NKJV

He who is slothful in his work Is a brother to him who is a great destroyer.

Proverbs 18:9 NKJV

House and riches are the inheritance of fathers: and a prudent wife is from the Lord.

Slothfulness casteth into a deep sleep; and an idle soul shall suffer hunger.

Proverbs 19:14-15

Whoever is kind to the poor lends to the Lord, and he will reward them for what they have done.

Proverbs 19:17 NIV

The fear of the Lord tendeth to life: and he that hath it shall abide satisfied; he shall not be visited with evil.

A slothful man hideth his hand in his bosom, and will not so much as bring it to his mouth again.

Proverbs 19:23-24

The righteous lead blameless lives; blessed are their children after them.

Proverbs 20:7 NIV

Do not love sleep, lest you come to poverty; Open your eyes, and you will be satisfied with bread.

Proverbs 20:13 NKJV

The thoughts of the diligent tend only to plenteousness; but of every one that is hasty only to want.

Proverbs 21:5

Whoever ignores the poor when they cry for help will also cry for help and not be answered.

Proverbs 21:13 NCV

He who loves pleasure will be a poor man; He who loves wine and oil will not be rich.

Proverbs 21:17 NKJV

The wise man saves for the future, but the foolish man spends whatever he gets.

Proverbs 21:20 TLB

A good name is rather to be chosen than great riches, and lov ing favor rather than silver and gold.

The rich and poor meet together; the Lord is the Maker of them all.

The reward of humility and the reverent and worshipful fear of the Lord is riches and honor and life.

Proverbs 22: 1-2, 4 AMP

The rich ruleth over the poor, and the borrower is servant to the lender.

Proverbs 22:7

He that hath a bountiful eye shall be blessed; for he giveth of his bread to the poor.

Proverbs 22:9

One who oppresses the poor to increase his wealth and one who gives gifts to the rich—both come to poverty.

Proverbs 22:16 NIV

Do you see someone skilled in their work? They will serve before kings; they will not serve before officials of low rank.

Proverbs 22:29 NIV

Don't weary yourself trying to get rich. Why waste your time? For riches can disappear as though they had the wings of a bird!

Proverbs 23:4-5 TLB

For the drunkard and the glutton will come to poverty, and drowsiness will clothe a man with rags.

Proverbs 23:21 NKJV

A house is built by wisdom and becomes strong through good sense. Through knowledge its rooms are filled with all sorts of precious riches and valuables.

Proverbs 24:3-4 NLT

I went by the field of the slothful, and by the vineyard of the man void of understanding;

And, lo, it was all grown over with thorns, and nettles had covered the face thereof, and the stone wall thereof was broken down.

Then I saw, and considered it well: I looked upon it, and received instruction.

Yet a little sleep, a little slumber, a little folding of the hands to sleep: So shall thy poverty come as one that travelleth; and thy want as an armed man.

Proverbs 24:30-34

He that covereth his sins shall not prosper: but whoso confesseth and forsaketh them shall have mercy.

Proverbs 28:13

Hard work brings prosperity; playing around brings poverty.

The man who wants to do right will get a rich reward. But the man who wants to get rich quick will quickly fail.

Giving preferred treatment to rich people is a clear case of selling one's soul for a piece of bread.

Trying to get rich quick is evil and leads to poverty.

He who is of a greedy spirit stirs up strife, but he who puts his trust in the Lord shall be enriched and blessed.

Proverbs 28:19-22 TLB

The one who trusts the Lord will succeed.

Proverbs 28:25 NCV

Those who give to the poor will lack nothing, but those who close their eyes to them receive many curses.

Proverbs 28:27 NIV

The king that faithfully judgeth the poor, his throne shall be established for ever.

Proverbs 29:14

That each of them may eat and drink, and find satisfaction in all their toil—this is the gift of God.

Ecclesiastes 3:13 NIV

Whoever loves money never has enough; whoever loves wealth is never satisfied with their income. This too is meaningless.

Ecclesiastes 5:10 NIV

Every man also to whom God hath given riches and wealth, and hath given him power to eat thereof, and to take his portion, and to rejoice in his labour; this is the gift of God.

Ecclesiastes 5:19

"If you become willing and obey me, you will eat good crops from the land. But if you refuse to obey and if you turn against me, you will be destroyed by your enemies' swords." The Lord himself said these things.

Isaiah 1:19-20 NCV

He will also send you rain for the seed you sow in the ground, and the food that comes from the land will be rich and plentiful.

Isaiah 20:23

I give waters in the wilderness, and rivers in the desert, to give drink to my people, my chosen.

Isaiah 43:20

I will go before you and make the crooked places straight; I will break in pieces the gates of bronze and cut the bars of iron.

I will give you the treasures of darkness and hidden riches of secret places, that you may

know that I, the Lord, Who call you by your name, am the God of Israel.

Isaiah 45:2-3 NKJV

I, even I, have foretold it; yes, I have called him [Cyrus]; I have brought him, and [the Lord] shall make his way prosperous.

Isaiah 48:15 AMP

Thus saith the Lord, thy Redeemer, the Holy One of Israel; I am the Lord thy God which teacheth thee to profit, which leadeth thee by the way that thou shouldest go.

Isaiah 48:17

Is not this the kind of fasting I have chosen: to loose the chains of injustice and untie the cords of the yoke, to set the oppressed free and break every yoke?

Is it not to share your food with the hungry and to provide the poor wanderer with shelter—when you see the naked, to clothe them,

and not to turn away from your own flesh and blood?

Then your light will break forth like the dawn, and your healing will quickly appear; then your righteousness will go before you, and the glory of the Lord will be your rear guard.

Then you will call, and the Lord will answer; you will cry for help, and he will say: Here am I.

If you do away with the yoke of oppression, with the pointing finger and malicious talk,

and if you spend yourselves in behalf of the hungry and satisfy the needs of the oppressed, then your light will rise in the darkness, and your night will become like the noonday.

The Lord will guide you always; he will satisfy your needs in a sun-scorched land and will strengthen your frame. You will be like a well-watered garden, like a spring whose waters never fail.

Your people will rebuild the ancient ruins and will raise up the age-old foundations;

you will be called Repairer of Broken Walls, Restorer of Streets with Dwellings.

If you keep your feet from breaking the Sabbath and from doing as you please on my holy day, if you call the Sabbath a delight and the Lord's holy day honorable, and if you honor it by not going your own way and not doing as you please or speaking idle words, then you will find your joy in the Lord, and I will cause you to ride in triumph on the heights of the land and to feast on the inheritance of your father Jacob." For the mouth of the Lord has spoken.

Isaiah 58:6-14 NIV

Arise [from the depression and prostration in which circumstances have kept you—rise to a new life]! Shine (be radiant with the glory of the Lord), for your light has come, and the glory of the Lord has risen upon you!

For behold, darkness shall cover the earth, and dense darkness [all] peoples, but the Lord shall arise upon you [O Jerusalem], and His glory shall be seen on you.

And nations shall come to your light, and kings to the brightness of your rising.

Then you shall see and be radiant, and your heart shall thrill and tremble with joy [at the glorious deliverance] and be enlarged; because the abundant wealth of the [Dead] Sea shall be turned to you, unto you shall the nations come with their treasures.

Isaiah 60:1-3,5 AMP

Unlike the past, invaders will not take their houses and confiscate their vineyards. For my people will live as long as trees, and my chosen ones will have time to enjoy their hard-won gains.

They will not work in vain, and their children will not be doomed to misfortune. For they are people blessed by the Lord, and their children, too, will be blessed.

Isaiah 65:22-23 NLT

Blessed is the man who trusts in the Lord, and whose hope is the Lord.

For he shall be like a tree planted by the waters, which spreads out its roots by the river, and will not fear when heat comes; But its leaf will be green, and will not be anxious in the year of drought, nor will cease from yielding fruit.

Jeremiah 17:7-8 NKJV

"He defended the cause of the poor and needy, and so all went well. Is that not what it means to know me?" declares the Lord.

Jeremiah 22:16 NIV

For I know the plans I have for you," declares the Lord, "plans to prosper you and not to harm you, plans to give you hope and a future.

Jeremiah 29:11 NIV

Behold, therefore, I beat My fists at the dishonest profit which you have made, and at the bloodshed which has been in your midst.

Ezekiel 22:13 NKJV

And you will live in Israel, the land I gave your ancestors long ago. You will be my people, and I will be your God.

I will cleanse you of your filthy behavior. I will give you good crops of grain, and I will send no more famines on the land.

I will give you great harvests from your fruit trees and fields, and never again will the surrounding nations be able to scoff at your land for its famines.

Ezekiel 36:28-30 NLT

So be happy, people of Jerusalem; be joyful in the Lord your God. Because he does what is right, he has brought you rain; he has sent the fall rain and the spring rain for you, as before.

And the threshing floors will be full of grain;

the barrels will overflow with new wine and olive oil.

Though I sent my great army against you—those swarming locusts and hopping locusts, the destroying locusts and the cutting locusts that ate your crops—I will pay you back for those years of trouble.

Then you will have plenty to eat and be full. You will praise the name of the Lord your God, who has done miracles for you. My people will never again be shamed.

Joel 2:23-26 NCV

For the seed shall be prosperous; the vine shall give her fruit, and the ground shall give her increase, and the heavens shall give their dew; and I will cause the remnant of this people to possess all these things.

Zechariah 8:12

Will a man rob God? Yet ye have robbed me. But ye say, Wherein have we robbed thee? In tithes and offerings.

Ye are cursed with a curse: for ye have robbed me, even this whole nation.

Bring ye all the tithes into the storehouse, that there may be meat in mine house, and prove me now herewith, saith the Lord of hosts, if I will not open you the windows of heaven, and pour you out a blessing, that there shall not be room enough to receive it.

And I will rebuke the devourer for your sakes, and he shall

not destroy the fruits of your ground; neither shall your vine cast her fruit before the time in the field, saith the Lord of hosts.

And all nations shall call you blessed: for ye shall be a delightsome land, saith the Lord of hosts.

Malachi 3:8-12

FINANCES SCRIPTURES
NEW TESTAMENT

Thy kingdom come, Thy will be done in earth, as it is in heaven.

Give us this day our daily bread.

Matthew 6:10-11

Don't store up treasures here on earth, where moths eat them and rust destroys them, and where thieves break in and steal.

Store your treasures in heaven, where moths and rust cannot destroy, and thieves do not break in and steal.

Wherever your treasure is, there the desires of your heart will also be.

Matthew 6:19-21 NLT

Therefore I say to you, do not worry about your life, what you will eat or what you will drink; nor about your body, what you will put on. Is not life more than food and the body more than clothing?

Look at the birds of the air, for they neither sow nor reap nor gather into barns; yet your heavenly Father feeds them. Are you not of more value than they?

Which of you by worrying can add one cubit to his stature?

So why do you worry about clothing? Consider the lilies of the field, how they grow: they neither toil nor spin; and yet I say to you that even Solomon in all his glory was not arrayed like one of these.

Now if God so clothes the grass of the field, which today is, and tomorrow is thrown into the oven, will He not much more clothe you, O you of little faith?

Therefore do not worry, saying, 'What shall we eat?' or 'What shall we drink?' or 'What shall we wear?'

For after all these things the Gentiles seek. For your heavenly Father knows that you need all these things.

But seek first the kingdom of God and His righteousness, and all these things shall be added to you.

Matthew 6:25-33 NKJV

But the seed falling on good soil refers to someone who hears the word and understands it. This is the one who produces a crop, yielding a hundred, sixty or thirty times what was sown.

Matthew 13:23 NIV

Then when they arrived at Capernaum the Temple tax-collectors came up and said to Peter, "Your master doesn't pay Temple-tax, we presume?"

"Oh, yes, he does!" replied Peter. Later when he went into the house Jesus anticipated what he was going to say. "What do you think, Simon?" he said. "Whom do the kings of this world get their rates and taxes from—their own people or from others?"

"From others," replied Peter.

"Then the family is exempt," Jesus told him. "Yet we don't want to give offence to these people, so go down to the lake and throw in your hook. Take the first fish that bites, open his mouth and you'll find a coin. Take that and give it to them, for both of us."

Matthew 17:24-27 Phillips

In that way the kingdom of heaven is like

this. A king was ready to finish his business with his servants.

The first servant was brought in. He owed the king a very large sum of money.

He could not pay it. So his master said, "Go sell him, his wife, his children, and everything he has, and pay me!"

So the servant bowed down in front of him. He begged, "Sir,

give me time. I will pay everything."

His master was sorry for him and let him go. He did not make him pay the money.

That same servant went out and met another servant. This man owed him a much smaller sum of money. He caught him by the throat and said, "Pay me what you owe me!"

Then this servant bowed down in front of him. He begged, "Give me time. I will pay you."

But he said, "No." He went and put the man in prison until he could pay what he owed him.

The other servants saw what he did. They were very sad. They went and told their master everything that had been done.

Then his master called the first servant to him. He said, "You bad man! I let you go. I did not make you pay all you owed me, because you begged me to be kind to you.

You should have been kind to the other servant, as I was kind to you."

His master was very angry. He turned the servant over to the prison guards until he could pay all he owed him.

That is like what my Father in heaven will do to every one of you, if you do not forgive your brother from your heart.

Matthew 18:23-35 WE

A man came to Jesus and asked, "Teacher, what good thing must I do to have life forever?"

Jesus answered, "Why do you ask me about what is good? Only God is good. But if you want to have life forever, obey the commands."

The man asked, "Which commands?"

Jesus answered, "You must not murder anyone; you must not be guilty of adultery; you must not steal; you must not tell lies about your neighbor; honor your father and mother; and love your neighbor as you love yourself."

The young man said, "I have obeyed all these things. What else do I need to do?"

Jesus answered, "If you want to be perfect, then go and sell your possessions and give the money to the poor. If you do this, you will have treasure in heaven. Then come and follow me."

But when the young man heard this, he left sorrowfully, because he was rich.

Then Jesus said to his followers, "I tell you the truth, it will be hard for a rich person to enter the kingdom of heaven.

Yes, I tell you that it is easier for a camel to go through the eye of a needle than for a rich person to enter the kingdom of God."

When Jesus' followers heard this, they were very surprised and asked, "Then who can be saved?"

Jesus looked at them and said, "For people this is impossible, but for God all things are possible."

Matthew 19:16-26 NCV

For the kingdom of heaven is like a man traveling to a far country, who called his own servants and delivered his goods to them.

And to one he gave five talents, to another two, and to another one, to each according to his own ability; and immediately he went on a journey.

Then he who had received the five talents went and traded with them, and made another five talents.

And likewise he who had received two gained two more also.

But he who had received one went and dug in the ground, and hid his lord's money.

After a long time the lord of those servants came and settled accounts with them.

So he who had received five talents came and brought five other talents, saying, 'Lord, you delivered to me five talents; look, I have gained five more talents besides them.'

His lord said to him, 'Well done, good and faithful servant;

you were faithful over a few things, I will make you ruler over many things. Enter into the joy of your lord.'

He also who had received two talents came and said, 'Lord, you delivered to me two talents; look, I have gained two more talents besides them.'

His lord said to him, 'Well done, good and faithful servant; you have been faithful over a few things, I will make you ruler over many things. Enter into the joy of your lord.'

Then he who had received the one talent came and said, 'Lord, I knew you to be a hard man, reaping where you have not sown, and gathering where you have not scattered seed.

And I was afraid, and went and hid your talent in the ground. Look, there you have what is yours.'

But his lord answered and said to him, 'You wicked and lazy servant, you knew that I reap where I have not sown, and gather where I have not scattered seed. So you ought to have deposited my money with the bankers, and at my coming I would have received back my own with interest.

Therefore take the talent from him, and give it to him who has ten talents. For to everyone who has, more will be given, and he will have abundance; but from him who does not have, even what he has will be taken away.'

Matthew 25:14-29 NKJV

But they think about the things of this world. They want to get money and other things to be happy. These things push the message out of their hearts. No good comes from it.

Mark 4:19 WE

And Jesus answered and said, Verily I say unto you, There is no man that hath left house, or brethren, or sisters, or father, or mother, or wife, or children, or lands, for my sake, and the gospel's, but he shall receive an hundredfold now in this time, houses, and brethren, and sisters, and mothers, and children, and lands, with persecutions; and in the world to come eternal life.

Mark 10:29-30

"Have faith in God," Jesus answered. "Truly I tell you, if anyone says to this mountain, 'Go, throw yourself into the sea,' and does not doubt in their heart but believes that what they say will happen, it will be done for them. Therefore I tell you, whatever you ask for in prayer, believe that you have received it, and it will be yours."

Mark 11:22-24 NIV

Jesus sat down in the temple near the place where people put in their money. He saw how the people put in money. Many rich people put in much money.

A poor woman, whose husband was dead, came. She put in two small pieces of money.

Jesus called his disciples. He said, `I tell you the truth. This poor woman has given more money than all the other people.

All these people had plenty of money and they gave only a part of it. She was poor and she gave everything she had. She has nothing left to live on.'

Mark 12:41-44 WE

One day the people were crowding closely round Jesus to hear God's message, as he stood on the shore of Lake Gennesaret. Jesus noticed two boats drawn up on the beach, for the fishermen had left them there while they were cleaning their nets. He went aboard one of the boats, which belonged to Simon, and asked him to push out a little from the shore. Then he sat down and continued his teach-ing of the crowds from the boat.

When he had finished speaking, he said to Simon, "Push out now into deep water and let down your nets for a catch."

279

Simon replied, "Master! We've worked all night and never caught a thing, but if you say so, I'll let the nets down."

And when they had done this, they caught an enormous shoal of fish—so big that the nets began to tear. So they signalled to their friends in the other boats to come and help them. They came and filled both the boats to sinking point.

Luke 5:1-7 Phillips

Give and men will give to you—yes, good measure, pressed down, shaken together and running over will they pour into your lap. For whatever measure you use with other people, they will use in their dealings with you."

Luke 6:38 Phillips

Then Jesus answered and said: "A certain man went down from Jerusalem to Jericho, and fell among thieves, who stripped him of his clothing, wounded him, and departed, leaving him half dead.

"Now by chance a certain priest came down that road. And when he saw him, he passed by on the other side.

"Likewise a Levite, when he arrived at the place, came and looked, and passed by on the other side.

"But a certain Samaritan, as he journeyed, came where he was. And when he saw him, he had compassion.

"So he went to him and bandaged his wounds, pouring on oil and wine; and he set him on his own animal, brought him to an inn, and took care of him.

"On the next day, when he departed, he took out two denarii, gave them to the innkeeper, and said to him, 'Take care of him; and whatever more you spend, when I come again, I will repay you.'

"So which of these three do you think was neighbor to him who fell among the thieves?"

And he said, "He who showed mercy on him."

Then Jesus said to him, "Go and do likewise."

Luke 10:30-37 NKJV

What sorrow awaits you Pharisees! For you are careful to tithe even the tiniest income from your herb gardens, but you ignore justice and the love of God. You should tithe, yes, but do not neglect the more important things.

Luke 11:42 NLT

Then he said to them, "Watch out! Be on your guard against all kinds of greed; life does not consist in an abundance of possessions."

And he told them this parable: "The ground of a certain rich man yielded an abundant harvest.

He thought to himself, 'What shall I do? I have no place to store my crops.'

"Then he said, 'This is what I'll do. I will tear down my barns and build bigger ones, and there I will store my surplus grain.

And I'll say to myself, "You have plenty of grain laid up for many years. Take life easy; eat, drink and be merry."'

"But God said to him, 'You fool! This very night your life will be demanded from you. Then who will get what you have prepared for yourself?'

"This is how it will be with whoever stores up things for them selves but is not rich toward God."

Luke 12:15-21 NIV

So Jesus, raising his eyes and seeing a great crowd on the way towards him, said to Philip, "Where can we buy food for these people to eat?" (He said this to test Philip, for he himself knew what he was going to do.)

"Ten pounds' worth of bread would not be enough for them," Philip replied, "even if they had only a little each."

Then Andrew, Simon Peter's brother, another disciple, put in, "There is a boy here who has five small barley loaves and a couple of fish, but what's the good of that for such a crowd?"

Then Jesus said, "Get the people to sit down." There was plenty of grass there, and the men, some five thousand of them, sat down. Then Jesus took the loaves, gave thanks for them and distributed them to the people sitting on the grass, and he distributed the fish in the same way, giving them as much as they wanted. When they had eaten enough, Jesus said to his disciples, "Collect the pieces that are left over so that nothing is wasted."

So they did as he suggested and filled twelve baskets with the broken pieces of the five barley loaves, which were left over after the people had eaten!

John 6:5-13 Phillips

A thief is only there to steal and kill and destroy. I came so they can have real and eternal life, more and better life than they ever dreamed of.

John 10:10 MSG

Afterward Jesus appeared again to his disciples, by the Sea of Galilee. It happened this way:

Simon Peter, Thomas (also known as Didymus), Nathanael from Cana in Galilee, the sons of Zebedee, and two other disciples were together. "I'm going out to fish," Simon Peter told them, and they said, "We'll go with you." So they went out and got into the boat, but that night they caught nothing.

Early in the morning, Jesus stood on the shore, but the disciples did not realize that it was Jesus.

He called out to them, "Friends, haven't you any fish?"

"No," they answered.

He said, "Throw your net on the right side of the boat and you will find some." When they did, they were unable to haul the net in because of the large number of fish.

Then the disciple whom Jesus loved said to Peter, "It is the Lord!" As soon as Simon Peter heard him say, "It is the Lord," he wrapped his outer garment around him (for he had taken it off) and jumped into the water. The other disciples followed in the boat, towing the net full of fish, for they were not far from shore, about a hundred yards. When they landed, they saw a fire of burning coals there with fish on it, and some bread.

Jesus said to them, "Bring some of the fish you have just

caught."

So Simon Peter climbed back into the boat and dragged the net ashore. It was full of large fish, 153, but even with so many the net was not torn. Jesus said to them, "Come and have breakfast." None of the disciples dared ask him, "Who are you?" They knew it was the Lord. Jesus came, took the bread and gave it to them, and did the same with the fish. This was now the third time Jesus appeared to his disciples after he was raised from the dead.

John 21:1-14 NIV

And with great power the apostles gave witness to the resurrection of the Lord Jesus. And great grace was upon them all. Nor was there anyone among them who lacked; for all who were possessors of lands or houses sold them, and brought the proceeds of the things that were sold, and laid them at the apostles' feet; and they distributed to each as anyone had need.

And Joses, who was also named Barnabas by the apostles (which is translated Son of Encouragement), a Levite of the country of Cyprus, having land, sold it, and brought the money and laid it at the apostles' feet.

Acts 4:33-37 NKJV

At Caesarea there was a man named Cornelius, a centurion in what was known as the Italian Regiment. He and all his family were devout and God-fearing; he gave generously to those in need and prayed to God regularly. One day at about three in the afternoon he had a vision. He distinctly saw an angel of God, who came to him and said, "Cornelius!"

Cornelius stared at him in fear. "What is it, Lord?" he asked.

The angel answered, "Your prayers and gifts to the poor have come up as a memorial offering before God."

Acts 10: 1-4 NIV

And now, brethren, I commend you to God, and to the word of his grace, which is able to build you up, and to give you an inheritance among all them which are sanctified.

I have coveted no man's silver, or gold, or apparel. Yea, ye yourselves know, that these hands

have ministered unto my necessities, and to them that were with me.

I have shewed you all things, how that so labouring ye ought to support the weak, and to remember the words of the Lord Jesus, how he said, It is more blessed to give than to receive.

Acts 20:32-35

The holy writings say, "No eye has seen the things God has made ready for those who love him. No ear has heard about them. No person's heart has ever thought of them."

1 Corinthians 2:9 WE

On the first [day] of each week, let each one of you [personally] put aside something and save it up as he has prospered [in proportion to what he is given], so that no collections will need to be taken after I come.

And when I arrive, I will send on those whom you approve and authorize with credentials to carry your gift [of charity] to Jerusalem.

1 Corinthians 16:2-3 AMP

But this I say, He which soweth sparingly shall reap also sparingly; and he which soweth bountifully shall reap also bountifully.

Every man according as he purposeth in his heart, so let him give; not grudgingly, or of necessity: for God loveth a cheerful giver.

And God is able to make all grace abound toward you; that ye, always having all sufficiency in all things, may abound to every good work:

(As it is written, He hath dispersed abroad; he hath given to the poor: his righteousness remaineth for ever. Now he that ministereth seed to the sower both minister bread for your food, and multiply your seed sown, and increase the fruits of your righteousness;)

Being enriched in every thing to all bountifulness, which causeth through us thanksgiving to God.

For the administration of this service not only supplieth the want of the saints, but is abundant also by many thanksgivings unto God.

2 Corinthians 9:6-12

So all who put their faith in Christ share the same blessing Abraham received because of his faith.

But those who depend on the law to make them right with God are under his curse, for the Scriptures say, "Cursed is everyone who does not observe and obey all the commands that are written in God's Book of the Law." So it is clear that no one can be made right with God by trying to keep the law. For the Scriptures say, "It is through faith that a righteous person has life." This way of faith is very different from the way of law, which says, "It is through obeying the law that a person has life." But Christ has rescued us from the curse pronounced by the law. When he was hung on the cross, he took upon himself the curse for our wrongdoing. For it is written in the Scriptures, "Cursed is everyone who is hung on a tree." Through Christ Jesus, God has blessed the Gentiles with the same blessing he promised to Abraham, so that we who are believers might receive the promised Holy Spirit through faith.

And now that you belong to Christ, you are the true children of Abraham. You are his heirs, and God's promise to Abraham belongs to you.

Galatians 3:9-14, 29 NLT

Do not be fooled: You cannot cheat God. People harvest only what they plant. If they plant to satisfy their sinful selves, their sinful selves will bring them ruin. But if they plant to please the Spirit, they will receive eternal life from the Spirit. We must not become tired of doing good.

We will receive our harvest of eternal life at the right time if we do not give up. When we have the opportunity to help anyone, we should do it. But we should give special attention to those who are in the family of believers.

Galatians 6:7-10 NCV

Let him that stole steal no more: but rather let him labour, working with his hands the thing which is good, that he may have to give to him that needeth.

Ephesians 4:28

I rejoiced greatly in the Lord that at last you renewed your concern for me. Indeed, you were concerned, but you had no opportunity to show it.

I am not saying this because I am in need, for I have learned to be content whatever the circumstances. I know what it is to be in need, and I know what it is to have plenty. I have learned the secret of being content in any and every situation, whether well fed or hungry, whether living in plenty or in want.

I can do all this through him who gives me strength.

Yet it was good of you to share in my troubles.

Moreover, as you Philippians know, in the early days of your acquaintance with the gospel, when I set out from Macedonia, not one church shared with me in the matter of giving and receiving, except you only; for even when I was in Thessalonica, you sent me aid more than once when I was in need.

Not that I desire your gifts; what I desire is that more be credited to your account.

I have received full payment and have more than enough. I am amply supplied, now that I have received from Epaphroditus the gifts you sent. They are a fragrant offering, an acceptable sacrifice, pleasing to God.

And my God will meet all your needs according to the riches of his glory in Christ Jesus.

Philippians 4:10-19 NIV

Brothers and sisters, by the authority of our Lord Jesus Christ we command you to stay away from any believer who refuses to work and does not follow the teaching we gave you.

You yourselves know that you should live as we live. We were not lazy when we were with you.

And when we ate another person's food, we always paid for it. We worked very hard night and day so we would not be an expense to any of you. We had the right to ask you to help us, but we worked to take care of ourselves so we would be an example for you to follow.

When we were with you, we gave you this rule: "Anyone who refuses to work should not eat."

We hear that some people in your group refuse to work. They do nothing but busy themselves in other people's lives.

We command those people and beg them in the Lord Jesus Christ to work quietly and earn their own food.

2 Thessalonians 3:6-12 NCV

But if anyone does not provide for his own, and especially for those of his household, he has denied the faith and is worse than an unbeliever.

1 Timothy 5:8 NKJV

But godliness with contentment is great gain. For we brought nothing into the world, and we can take nothing out of it. But if we have food and clothing, we will be content with that.

Those who want to get rich fall into temptation and a trap and into many foolish and harmful desires that plunge people into ruin and destruction.

For the love of money is a root of all kinds of evil. Some people, eager for money, have wandered from the faith and pierced themselves with many griefs.

1 Timothy 6:6-10 NIV

Command those who are rich in this present world not to be arrogant nor to put their hope in wealth, which is so uncertain, but to put their hope in God, who richly provides us with every thing for our enjoyment. Command them to do good, to be rich in good deeds, and to be generous and willing to share. In this way they will lay up treasure for themselves as a firm foundation for the coming age, so that they may take hold of the life that is truly life.

1 Timothy 6:17-19 NIV

For this Melchizedek, king of Salem, priest of the Most High God, who met Abraham returning from the slaughter of the kings and blessed him, to whom also Abraham gave a tenth part of all, first being translated "king of righteousness," and then also king of Salem, meaning "king of peace," without father, without mother, without genealogy, having neither beginning of days nor end of life, but made like the Son of God, remains a priest continually.

Now consider how great this man was, to whom even the patriarch Abraham gave a tenth of the spoils.

And indeed those who are of the sons of Levi, who receive the priesthood, have a commandment to receive tithes from the people according to the law, that is, from their brethren, though

293

they have come from the loins of Abraham; but he whose gene-alogy is not derived from them received tithes from Abraham and blessed him who had the promises.

Now beyond all contradiction the lesser is blessed by the better.

Here mortal men receive tithes, but there he receives them, of whom it is witnessed that he lives. For it is evident that our Lord arose from Judah, of which tribe Moses spoke nothing concerning priesthood.

And it is yet far more evident if, in the likeness of Melchize-dek, there arises another priest who has come, not according to the law of a fleshly commandment, but according to the power of an endless life. By so much more Jesus has become a surety of a better covenant.

Hebrews 7:1-8, 14-16, 22 NKJV

Beloved, I wish above all things that thou mayest prosper and be in health, even as thy soul prospereth.

3 John 2

After this I looked, and, behold, a door was opened in heaven: and the first voice which I heard was as it were of a trumpet talking with me; which said, Come up hither, and I will shew thee things which must be hereafter.

And immediately I was in the spirit: and, behold, a throne was set in heaven, and one sat on the throne.

And he that sat was to look upon like a jasper and a sardine stone: and there was a rainbow round about the throne, in sight like unto an emerald.

And round about the throne were four and twenty seats: and upon the seats I saw four and twenty elders sitting, clothed in white raiment; and they had on their heads crowns of gold.

Revelation 4:1-4

He who overcomes shall inherit all things, and I will be his God and he shall be My son.

Revelation 21:7 NKJV

The wall was made of jasper, and the city was pure gold, as clear as glass.

The wall of the city was built on foundation stones inlaid with twelve precious stones: the first was jasper, the second sapphire, the third agate, the fourth emerald, the fifth onyx, the sixth carnelian, the seventh chrysolite, the eighth beryl, the ninth topaz, the tenth chrysoprase, the eleventh jacinth, the twelfth amethyst.

The twelve gates were made of pearls—each gate from a single pearl! And the main street was pure gold, as clear as glass.

Revelation 21:18-21 NLT

Look, I am coming soon! My reward is with me, and I will give to each person according to what they have done.

I am the Alpha and the Omega, the First and the Last, the Beginning and the End.

Blessed are those who wash their robes, that they may have the right to the tree of life and may go through the gates into the city.

Revelation 22:12-14 NIV

PRAYER OF SALVATION

God loves you—no matter who you are, no matter what your past. God loves you so much that He gave His one and only begotten Son for you. The Bible tells us that "...whoever believes in Him shall not perish but have eternal life" (John 3:16 NIV). Jesus laid down His life and rose again so that we could spend eternity with Him in heaven and experience His absolute best on earth. If you would like to receive Jesus into your life, say the following prayer out loud and mean it from your heart.

Heavenly Father, I come to You admitting that I am a sinner. Right now, I choose to turn away from sin, and I ask You to cleanse me of all unrighteousness. I believe that Your Son, Jesus, died on the cross to take away my sins. I also believe that He rose again from the dead so that I might be forgiven of my sins and made righteous through faith in Him. I call upon the name of Jesus Christ to be the Savior and Lord of my life. Jesus, I choose to follow You and ask that You fill me with the power of the Holy Spirit. I declare that right now I am a child of God. I am free from sin and full of the right-eousness of God. I am saved in Jesus' name. Amen.

If you prayed this prayer to receive Jesus Christ as your Savior for the first time, please contact us on the Web at **www.harrisonhouse.com** to receive a free book.

Or you may write to us at

Harrison House • P.O. Box 35035 • Tulsa, Oklahoma 74153

Fast. Easy.
Convenient.

For the latest Harrison House product information and author news, look no further than your computer. All the details on our powerful, life-changing products are just a click away. New releases, E-mail subscriptions, testimonies, monthly specials—find it all in one place. Visit harrisonhouse.com today!

harrisonhouse

The Harrison House Vision

Proclaiming the truth and the power

Of the Gospel of Jesus Christ

With excellence;

Challenging Christians to

Live victoriously,

Grow spiritually,

Know God intimately.